BOEING

BOEING

an aircraft album

No. 4

KENNETH MUNSON

GORDON
SWANBOROUGH

Arco Publishing Company, Inc.
NEW YORK

Published by ARCO PUBLISHING COMPANY, INC.
219 Park Avenue South, New York, N.Y. 10003

First published 1972

Library of Congress Catalog Number 70–179696
ISBN 0–668–02582–4

Printed in Great Britain

Contents

Introduction

WILLIAM E. BOEING, whose name has been borne for more than half a century by one of the world's major aeronautical manufacturing companies, was born in Detroit, Michigan, on October 1, 1881, the son of a prosperous timber merchant. After graduating from Yale University in 1904, the young William Boeing spent the next five years training to enter the timber trade, and by the time that World War I broke out in Europe was successfully in business on his own account in Seattle, Washington.

On July 4, 1914, just one month before war broke out in Europe, William Boeing had his first experience of flying when he was taken up as a passenger in a Curtiss seaplane from nearby Lake Washington. Among his friends at that time was a US Navy officer, Commander G. Conrad Westervelt, then serving on attachment to a Seattle shipyard. During 1915 the two men often discussed the development of aviation in America and were convinced that, between them, they could improve upon the somewhat primitive aeroplanes that were still all too typical of current US designs.

Once they had agreed to work together on the design and construction of a new aeroplane, Boeing bought a specimen of the latest Martin two-seat seaplane, which was then one of the most modern types available in North America. A large building was erected on the shores of Lake Union, Seattle, both to house the Martin biplane and to serve as the workshop for building the new machine. The latter, named simply 'B & W' from the initials of its two builders, was designed during 1915–16, but by the time that it made its first flight in June 1916 the brief partnership had been ended by the transfer of Cmdr Westervelt to a new Navy post on the east coast. However, the successful early flights of the B & W encouraged Boeing to establish, with effect from July 15, 1916, the Pacific Aero Products Company especially for the manufacture of aeroplanes.

A new title, Boeing Airplane Company, was taken on April 26, 1917, shortly after the entry of the United States into World War I and the receipt of a Navy contract for 50 of the company's Type C two-seat training biplanes. Other wartime orders included one for a like quantity of Curtiss HS–2L flying-boats (later reduced to 25), and such contracts—large by the standards of the time—were clearly beyond the facilities available in the Lake Union building. New and larger premises were therefore obtained at the Heath shipyard, which lay south of Seattle on the Duwamish River, and these were further extended after the receipt of the HS–2L order. Neither facility included an airstrip: this was no great hindrance to the flight-testing of water-borne aircraft, although most of the early Boeing types were test-flown either at Sand Point, a Naval air

Facing page: *Production line of Boeing 707 jet transports.*

Above: *Original Lake Union Building of 1916, photographed about 1930.* [Peter M. Bowers collection

7

station about 10 miles to the north on the shore of Lake Washington, or at the Army field at Camp Lewis, some 50 miles from Seattle in the opposite direction. Not until 1928 did the company possess its own airfield, Boeing Field, renamed from the former King County Airport and situated only some two miles south-west of Seattle.

The wartime orders were sufficient to make the Boeing Airplane Company one of America's busiest aircraft manufacturers, but in the immediate post-war vacuum there was insufficient aircraft work to keep all of the staff fully employed. However, a force of trained carpenters and boat-builders in a flourishing timber-producing area was unlikely to be without some kind of work for very long, and Boeing's employees were able to mark time by building sea-going craft and furniture. The former included large floating sleds, from which a number of experiments were conducted in the launching of landplane aircraft.

Then, in 1921, came the company's largest contract so far, for 200 Thomas-Morse MB–3A fighters for the US Army. This was followed by others involving the building or conversion of large numbers of DH–4s, but Boeing had no intention of making a career solely out of building aeroplanes designed by other people. It was the MB–3A contract which sparked off the first significant post-war product of the company's own design. To undertake, at its own expense, the design and develop-

ment of a new fighter, at a time when the Army's fighter requirements were already filled, would itself have been enough of a gamble; allied to the decision also to adopt new design concepts and new constructional methods, it became doubly so. Taking a leaf out of Anthony Fokker's book, after studying the highly successful wartime D.VII fighter, Boeing designers decided to go for an arc-welded steel-tube fuselage (Fokker had used gas welding) and all-wood, near-cantilever wings with a thick aerofoil section.

The gamble may be said to have paid off handsomely, for the little PW–9 was to be the inspiration behind two families of biplane fighters, built extensively for the Army and Navy in the inter-war years, as well as the later P–26 monoplane series for the US Army. It is also worth remarking

that, from that point onward in its history, Boeing has frequently used aerofoil sections of its own design rather than the established Clark, NACA or other forms more commonly to be found elsewhere.

Incidental activities during the 1920s included associations with a number of famous non-Boeing aircraft. In 1924 the company furnished the interchangeable float landing gear used by the four Douglas World Cruisers on their round-the-world attempt; and in 1927–28 it converted Sir Hubert Wilkins' famous Polar Fokker trimotor, the *Detroiter*, into the even more celebrated *Southern Cross* used by Charles Kingsford Smith for his epic trans-Pacific flight of 1928.

While the development and production of military aircraft occupied a major portion of Boeing's resources during the

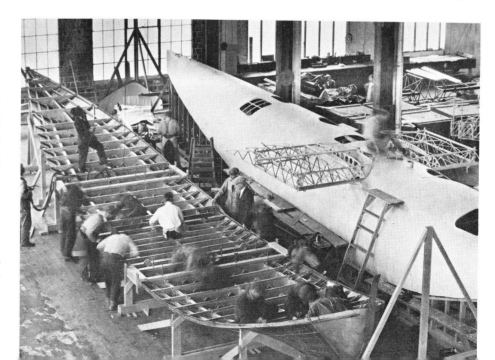

Wood-and-veneer upper and all-metal lower halves of the hull of the Boeing PB–1 flying-boat of 1925.

1920s and early 1930s, the company also kept its eye firmly on the civil market. Its big chance came in 1927, when the US Post Office threw open to industry the operation of the trans-continental mail services that had hitherto been government-operated. Boeing had in fact designed a mail-carrying aeroplane, the Model 40, two years before this, but it was unable to realise its potential performance with the heavy, water-cooled Liberty engine originally fitted. But by 1927, when it became possible to install an air-cooled radial engine—the Pratt & Whitney Wasp—of comparable power to the Liberty, William Boeing was able to claim that he had an aeroplane able to 'carry payload instead of radiators and water'. The Wasp-engined Model 40A was good enough to win for Boeing the San Francisco–Chicago mail

route, and a new company, Boeing Air Transport Inc, was formed to operate the service. It opened on July 1, 1927, and on July 26 the Model 40A became only the second American aircraft type to hold one of the newly-introduced Approved Type Certificates for unlimited commercial operation. (It was, incidentally, with the Model 40 that Boeing first introduced its Model-numbering sequence, earlier designs being allotted numbers retrospectively.)

The late 1920s marked a period of considerable commercial expansion for Boeing. The opening of Boeing Field, as the operational centre for Boeing Air Transport, was followed late in 1928 by the acquisition of Pacific Air Transport, whose routes were combined with those of BAT under the new collective title of The Boeing System. Also in 1928 the company formed

its own School of Aeronautics, based at Oakland, California. Operated initially as a subsidiary of BAT, the School remained a Boeing enterprise until 1934; it was taken over by the US Army in 1942. The year 1929 was a particularly active one: in February Boeing acquired the Hamilton Metalplane Company, and in the summer joined with the Hoffar-Breeching Shipyard of Vancouver, British Columbia, to set up a Canadian subsidiary, Boeing Aircraft of Canada Ltd, for the manufacture of selected Seattle designs. Later in the year came the biggest single expansion of all, when the entire Boeing organisation joined forces with Chance Vought Corporation, Hamilton Aero Manufacturing Company and Pratt & Whitney Aircraft Company under the 'umbrella' of a new holding company, United Aircraft and Transport Corporation, with headquarters at Hartford, Connecticut.

Each member of UATC continued its former activities under its own name, and in due course this parent corporation acquired, under similar conditions, three more manufacturing companies—Sikorsky Aviation Corporation, Stearman Aircraft Company and the Standard Steel Propeller Company—and three more transport operators—National Air Transport, Stout Airlines and Varney Air Lines. The Hamilton and Standard companies subsequently merged to become Hamilton-Standard, which today is one of the leading propeller manufacturers in the world. The

Structure assembly of the Boeing P–12 fighter, one of Boeing's most successful designs of the 1920s.

new UATC industrial giant was thus a self-contained organisation able to produce its own aeroplanes, aero-engines and propellers, and to operate them on its own far-ranging air routes. Indeed, the latter activity became large enough to be split off from the parent UATC, with the new name of United Air Lines.

The existence of the monolithic UATC was, however, short-lived. In the world-wide economic depression that followed the stock market collapse of 1929, aviation was as hard-hit as most other major industries. One outcome in the US was the 1934 Air Mail Act, under which aircraft and engine manufacturers were forbidden to hold interests in airlines with air mail contracts. When this became law a separate and independent United Air Lines Transport Corporation was formed, which also assumed responsibility for the Boeing School of Aeronautics. On the manufacturing side Hamilton-Standard, Pratt & Whitney, Sikorsky and Chance Vought formed themselves into a new United Aircraft Corporation. Boeing, with the Wichita-based Stearman company as a subsidiary, left the group to become, once again, an independent concern, adopting a minor name change to that of Boeing Aircraft Company. At this stage William Boeing departed from the company that he had founded. It had always been his declared intention to retire at the age of 50 and he had, in fact, withdrawn from active participation in UATC in August 1933. His final severing of all links with the organisation was, however, tinged with bitterness over the government's handling of the air mail contracts.

It is against this background that one must view a considerable amount of pioneering work by Boeing in aircraft design and construction. To break away from the traditional wood-and-fabric-covered biplanes of the times towards all-metal monoplanes, with or without such other then-radical features as cantilever wings and retractable undercarriages, would have been a courageous step under normal circumstances: under the un-settled economic conditions prevailing in the early 1930s it was remarkably so. Yet from the first tentative step—the conversion of a P-12 fighter biplane into the Model 202 monoplane, by the simple basic expedient of removing its lower wing—Boeing pursued a course that led to such then-revolutionary monoplane designs as the XP-9, Monomail, B-9, Model 247 and B-17 Flying Fortress.

The unpleasant political trends in Europe in the latter half of the 1930s opened a new period of expansion for the world's aviation industries that was to culminate in programmes of unprecedented size during World War II. So far as Boeing was concerned this expansion began in 1936, when a new factory (Plant 2) was built at Boeing Field to handle initial orders for the large, four-engined B-17 and Stratoliner. This later expanded in size proportionally to the wartime B-17 orders which followed. On April 8, 1939, the Stearman company, already a wholly-owned Boeing subsidiary, became its Wichita Division. Its facilities, too, were extended to meet increasing military orders for the Kaydet series of training biplanes developed by the original company. The number of employees at Seattle alone rose from 1,755 at the beginning of 1938 to 8,724 by August 1940; a month after the attack on Pearl Harbor the figure had leapt to 28,840.

The biggest single cause of this pheno-menal expansion was the Flying Fortress bomber, for, although initiated as an Army Air Corps requirement in 1934, it did not enter large-scale production until 1941. With the appearance of the B-17E and B-17F models, even the greatly-increased Boeing facilities were unable to produce the required quantities quickly enough, resulting in the creation of the B-V-D (Boeing - Vega - Douglas) manufacturing 'pool' to handle the programme.

In 1942 Boeing's production resources were taxed even further by the evolution of the B-29 Superfortress, 500 of which were already on order by the end of January. Again an industry-wide pro-duction pool was organised, and the Navy-built factory at Renton, on the south side of Lake Washington—erected originally to build the PBB-1 flying-boat—was allocated to Boeing for B-29 production; but the B-29 posed other problems besides sheer quantity. Moreover, the placing of such large orders meant that hundreds of B-29 airframe shells were completed before many of the systems or equipment instal-lations had been fully developed or tested. The result was the so-called 'Battle of Kansas', where in the Spring of 1944 the Army set up three modification centres to cope with this problem without hindering the main production flow. By January 1945, Boeing's personnel strength at Seattle reached a wartime peak of 44,754 employees.

Apart from its unique rôle in bringing about the end of World War II, the

The B–29 Enola Gay, *used to drop the first atomic bomb on Hiroshima in August 1945.*

Superfortress was also destined to give Boeing its first major grasp of the smaller post-war markets, military and civil. A little designation-juggling enabled a developed version, the B–50, to survive the inevitable post-war cutbacks in military contracts—a fact no doubt appreciated even more by the US Air Force when the Korean War broke out in 1950. Another B–29 development was the C–97, designed originally for a transport rôle but which, with the B–29 and B–50, was to begin what has since become almost a Boeing monopoly—that of providing flight refuelling tanker aircraft for the US Air Force. The C–97's commercial counterpart, the Stratocruiser, also made more of an impact in airline circles than its modest production total might suggest.

The post-war run-down was, inevitably, reflected in the size and strength of the company, which in early 1948 reverted to the title Boeing Airplane Company. The Seattle staff dwindled to around the 9,000 mark, and the Wichita and Renton plants were closed, though they were to be re-opened in 1948–50 for KB–29 conversion work and subsequent programmes.

The first of the latter concerned the B–47 Stratojet strategic bomber, an aeroplane as historic in its way as the Monomail or the B–17 before it. Production of the B–47 began at Wichita (the two prototypes having been Seattle-built), and eventually reached such proportions that the wartime B-V-D pool was re-established to meet the demands of the Korean War. Even more significantly, the B–47 established a basic design configuration that underlaid, with one exception, every subsonic jet aircraft type built by Boeing up to 1970. These have included the B–52 Stratofortress—perhaps the last global-range jet bomber of its size the world will ever see—the KC–135, and the family of commercial jet transports that has descended from the historic Boeing 707 prototype which first put its nose outside the hangar doors at Renton on May 14, 1954. The modest PanAm order for six Boeing 707s, placed in 1955, precipitated a transformation of the commercial transport scene which, by the end of its first 15 years, saw a total of around 3,600 jet airliners of all types in service throughout the world. Boeing has reaped a handsome proportion of this market, with civil orders for the 707, 720, 727, 737 and 747 totalling more than 2,200 by early 1971.

Happily, William Boeing was able to see the beginnings of this upward trend in company fortunes before his death, in Seattle, on September 28, 1956. Three and a half years later, in March 1960, the company diversified its list of aircraft products by acquiring Vertol Aircraft Corporation (the former Piasecki Helicopter Corporation) of Philadelphia. With Vertol established as a Boeing division, the company adopted its present, simplified name of The Boeing Company in May 1961.

The amount of jet transport business in the 1960s was well reflected in the size of the Seattle work force, which in mid-1968 was in the region of 105,000 employees. By two years later, however, when the initial waves of orders for the more recent types had settled down to a steadier rate, this figure had shrunk to some 55,000, with the prospect of a further reduction to around 45,000 by the end of 1970. Indeed, after riding the crest of the wave for a prolonged period—despite such major disappointments as the failure to gain the USAF's TFX and HCX contracts, now represented by the General Dynamics F–111 and the Lockheed C–5A Galaxy—the company found 1970 a critical year in many respects. It culminated in the Senate's refusal in March 1971 to continue backing development of the American supersonic transport, a blow which the award of the potentially lucrative AWACS military contract in mid-1970 could do little to offset.

Fortunately, although its major efforts are devoted to the production of aeroplanes,

Boeing has other strings to its bow. This album is concerned, essentially, with Boeing aircraft, but a brief mention of other company activities is helpful in providing an overall perspective.

Although no longer a current activity, Boeing supported for many years a Turbine Division at Seattle, the work of which dated from 1943 followed by the running of its first small gas-turbine engine three years later. Its main product was the T50 series of small two-shaft engines, of which more than 1,500 were built. Phasing-out of engine production began in 1966, and in 1969 all remaining rights in its aero-engine products were transferred to Steward-Davis Inc of Long Beach, California.

The Boeing Company today is divided into five basic sections: the Commercial Airplane Group, Aerospace Group, Military Aircraft Systems Division (formed 1968), Wichita Division and Vertol Division. Of these, the MASD was primarily concerned during the first year or so of its existence with the design competition for the B–1 supersonic bomber. The Aerospace Group, based at the company's space centre at Kent, Washington, about 12 miles south of Seattle, earlier produced the IM–99 Bomarc area-defence missile and is now responsible *inter alia* for the LGM-30 Minuteman ICBM and the AGM-69A SRAM (short-range attack missile) programmes.

This Group also makes a major contribution to the American spaceflight programmes. Since its formation, it has developed a number of different items of space 'hardware', among which one of the most promising projects (despite its cancel-

lation in 1963 by the USAF before the start of flight trials) was the X–20 Dyna-Soar single-seat lifting-body re-entry vehicle. Currently the Group is deeply involved in the Apollo programme, with responsibility for producing the S.1C first stage of the Saturn V launch rocket. Boeing's Burner upper-stage booster rockets have helped place a number of unmanned satellite vehicles in orbit, and the series of Lunar Orbiter spacecraft brought back close-up photographs of more than 99 per cent of the Moon's surface in preparation for the Apollo programme. During 1970 it began work on the Lunar Rover, a vehicle intended for transporting astronauts about the lunar surface. Non-aerospace activities include the development of hydrofoil craft, of which two types are in service with the US Navy.

The brief two-man partnership of 1915 has thus grown in its first half-century into

Test firing of an IM–99B Bomarc interceptor missile at Cape Canaveral (now Cape Kennedy), Florida.

one of the leading aerospace companies in the world, and one whose history has emphasised repeatedly its readiness to accept, and ability to overcome, the challenges of the fast-developing industry in which it serves. As it enters the 1970s, with subsonic jet transport orders falling off, each of its two largest US competitors already in the airbus market, the supersonic transport programme forfeited and the Apollo space programme curtailed, there can be no doubt that it faces a period as full of challenge as any in its past.

Authors' Note

THE PREPARATION of this album has been aided considerably by contributions from several people, among whom two are deserving of special mention. Peter M. Bowers of The Boeing Company, whose own definitive work *Boeing Aircraft since 1916* (Putnam & Co Ltd) was inevitably a valuable basis for this smaller volume, was kind enough to read and offer constructive comment upon the manuscript and to loan photographs from his personal collection; and Harold E. Carr, Boeing's News Bureau Manager, dealt patiently and courteously with requests for photographs and other material over a period of many months.

The production lists given in the following pages relate only to initial deliveries by Boeing, and do not record subsequent changes of ownership and/or identification markings. All photographs appearing in this album are by courtesy of The Boeing Company, unless otherwise acknowledged.

Aeroplane Types

Type B & W
(Model 1)

THE FIRST AEROPLANE with which William E. Boeing was associated was a two-seat biplane, the idea for which arose from informal conversations between Boeing and a colleague, Commander G. Conrad Westervelt of the US Navy. It was started as a private venture, design work beginning late in 1915 and clearly owing much to that of the Martin TA floatplane, an example of which was owned by Boeing at that time. The new aircraft, also a twin-float seaplane, was known simply as the B & W, from the initials of its originators. Two examples were built, and were assembled in the hangar-workshop on the shore of Lake Union, Seattle, where the Martin was also stored. By the time the first B & W (named *Bluebird*) made its maiden flight, on June 29, 1916, the Navy had transferred Cmdr Westervelt to a new post, leaving Boeing free to form a company, the Pacific Aero Products Company, to replace the original informal partnership. Both *Bluebird* and the second machine, *Mallard*, which flew in November 1916, performed satisfactorily, and sufficient interest in the design was shown by the US Navy to promote the development of an improved version

intended for the training of naval pilots. The two B & W machines were sold in 1918 to the New Zealand government, by whom they were used for air mail flying and training until about 1923.

The B & W exhibited typical design and constructional features for its day, being of fabric-covered wooden construction with unstaggered, unequal-span wings. Power plant was a 125hp Hall-Scott A–5 in-line engine. One novel—though short-lived—feature was the provision of a wheel-topped control column, the wheel actuating rudder movement while the column was moved forwards or sideways to actuate the elevators or ailerons respectively. The replacement of this by a more conventional system, and of the original floats by larger ones, were the only notable modifications made to the original design.

Top: *B & W biplane afloat near the original Lake Union building in 1916.*

Right: *The B & W 'replica', built in 1966 to commemorate the fiftieth anniversary of The Boeing Company.* [J. Hutchinson

In 1966, to mark the fiftieth anniversary of William Boeing's first company, a copy of the original B & W was built, although concessions to present-day structural requirements—increases in the size of the vertical tail and floats, and the use of a Lycoming GO–435 engine as the power plant—prohibit this from being classed as a true replica. Manufacture was undertaken by the Jobmaster Corporation, whose owner, Clayton L. Scott, was formerly a Boeing test pilot and personal pilot to William Boeing. The 'new' B & W, appropriately registered N1916L, made its first flight on May 25, 1966, and subsequently made a number of appearances in connection with various anniversary celebrations.

Specification

SPAN	52ft 0in
LENGTH	31ft 2in
WING AREA	580sq ft
GROSS WEIGHT	2,800lb
MAX SPEED	75mph
CRUISING SPEED	67mph
RANGE	320 miles

Production
Bluebird (no registration)
Mallard (no registration)
N1916L (replica, 1966)

Type C seaplanes
(Models 2, 3 and 5)

THE SYSTEM governing the designation of these early seaplanes is to some extent speculative. The first with a C designation was known as the C–4, apparently from combining the third letter of the alphabet —signifying that, including the Boeing-owned Martin seaplane, it was the third design used—with the figure 4 to indicate that it was the fourth aeroplane to be *owned* by Boeing. That it was the second design *originated* by Boeing is reflected in the Model number, which was applied retrospectively in 1925. Built while the company was still known as Pacific Aero Products, it had staggered wings, rigged with dihedral, and much-modified tail surfaces compared with the B & W. After completing its flight tests it was dismantled, but was rebuilt in August 1918,

redesignated C–11 and sold to a private customer.

Meanwhile, to the order of the US Navy, two examples had been completed of what was later identified as Model 3. These were designated C–5 and C–6, differing from the C–4 principally in having an inverted-Vee arrangement of the centre-section support struts instead of the latter's parallel arrangement. They were delivered shortly after the United States entered World War I in April 1917; evaluation was followed by an order for 50 basically similar machines for primary training, and one further test aircraft fitted with a Curtiss OXX–6 engine, a large central float and smaller stabilising floats under the lower wings. The latter was designated C–1F, but the trainers, utilising their Navy serial numbers, were individually designated from C–650 to C–699. All were given the Boeing Model number 5. Despite the unreliability of their

Model 2 (C–4) seaplane.

100hp Hall-Scott A–7A engines, the trainers served with the USN until the end of the war, when they were sold off as war surplus. Most of those bought were then refitted with a more reliable power plant, and at least two are known to have survived until 1931.

One final C-type (Model 5), built for William Boeing, was originally known as the C–700 and then, after refitting with an L–4 engine, as the CL–4S. With this machine Boeing and Edward Hubbard began, on March 3, 1919, the International Contract Air Mail Service between Seattle and Victoria, British Columbia.

Specification

SPAN	43ft 10in
LENGTH	27ft 0in
HEIGHT	12ft 7in
WING AREA	495sq ft
GROSS WEIGHT	2,395lb
MAX SPEED	73mph
CRUISING SPEED	65mph
RANGE	200 miles

Production
Model 2 (no registration)
Model 3 147–148 (USN)
       (plus one civil, no registration)
Model 5 650–699 (USN)
      A–4347 (USN)
      G–CADR (C–700)

Top: *Model 3 seaplane, with William Boeing's original Martin seaplane in background.*

Left: *William Boeing's C–700 (Model 5), after modification to CL–4S in 1918.*

15

Type EA
(Model 4)

INTERVENING in the sequence of C type seaplanes, the EA (two of which were built) was in essence a landplane adaptation of the Model 3, though it differed in a number of other major respects. The problematical Hall-Scott engine was replaced by the more reliable 90hp Curtiss OX-5; the overall wing span was increased by 5ft 0in, and aileron area increased; and side-by-side seating was provided for the two occupants instead of the separate tandem cockpits of the Model 3. A conventional wheel-and-tailskid landing gear was fitted, with a third, smaller wheel mounted ahead of the main pair to reduce the risk of a nose-over on landing. The two EAs were delivered for evaluation to the US Army (which probably accounts for the A in the designation) in January 1917, their purchase being regularised by the award of a sales contract three months later, after America's entry into World War I.

Specification

SPAN	48ft 10in
LENGTH	24ft 10in
WING AREA	479sq ft
GROSS WEIGHT	2,185lb
MAX SPEED	67mph
CRUISING SPEED	60mph
RANGE	280 miles

Production
536–537

Curtiss HS–2L

THE CURTISS HS–2L, evolved by combining the airframe of the earlier HS–1 with the ubiquitous 360hp Liberty engine, was the US Navy's standard flying-boat patrol bomber during America's participation in World War I. The Liberty was first flight-tested in an HS–1 on October 21, 1917, and contracts were subsequently placed for the manufacture of several hundred HS–1Ls. The designation HS–2L followed the introduction of a 12ft increase in wing span to permit the carriage of a heavier bomb load. Since the numbers required were more than could be handled

by Curtiss alone, several other US manufacturers, including Boeing, were brought into the building programme.

Boeing's original contract was for 50 of these flying-boats, a figure reduced to 25 after Armistice cancellations. The Boeing-built machines (to which no Model number was allocated) were distinguishable from all other HS–2Ls in having ailerons on the upper wings only. Experience gained during their construction stood the company in good stead in the development of its own post-war flying-boat designs, the B–1 and BB–1.

Specification

SPAN	74ft 1in
LENGTH	39ft 0in
HEIGHT	14ft 7in
WING AREA	803sq ft
GROSS WEIGHT	6,432lb
MAX SPEED	85mph
CRUISING SPEED	78mph
RANGE	575 miles

Production

A–4231 to A–4255
A–4256 to A–4280 (production cancelled)

B–1
(Models 6 and 204)

BOEING'S FIRST post-war (and hence first commercial) aeroplane design was the B–1, an attractive little three-seat pusher flying-boat with (at first) a 200hp Hall-Scott L–6 engine. It flew for the first time on December 27, 1919, and in 1920 followed the C–700 into operation with Edward Hubbard's International Contract Air Mail Service between Seattle and Victoria, BC. Before it was retired, in 1928, it had flown over 350,000 miles and worn out six engines.

The post-war glut of surplus military aircraft successfully precluded any further sales of the original B–1 design, but by 1928 these had largely been retired from service and two much-developed versions, the B–1D and B–1E, were produced. These had four-seat enclosed cabins, modified tail contours, and 220hp Wright J–5 or 410hp Pratt & Whitney Wasp radial engines instead of the Vee-type Liberty. Two Model 6Ds (B–1D) and six Model 6Es (B–1E) were built, making their first flights in April and March 1928 respectively;

but the structural redesign was such as to justify an entirely new Model number, and accordingly Model 204 was allocated to subsequent B–1Es. In these the seating capacity was increased to five, but only two examples were completed by Boeing —one, for William E. Boeing, being a 204A fitted with dual controls. Coincidentally, this was later used on another Seattle–Victoria air mail service, operated by Percy Barnes. The three remaining uncompleted Model 204s were bought by a private customer, who eventually completed one. Four others were, however, built by Boeing's Canadian factory—its first aircraft product—and were designated C–204 Thunderbird.

The original B–1 Model 6, after some depredation by vandals and the weather, was restored in 1951 and is now in the Museum of History and Industry in Seattle.

Boeing-Canada put to use the experience gained while building the Thunderbird by designing a monoplane development which was given the name Totem. Of high-wing layout, the Totem seated three passengers in addition to the pilot, and was

Above left: *Model 4 (Type EA), with main and 'anti-noseover' wheel landing gear.*

Left: *Absence of lower-wing ailerons identified the 25 Curtiss HS–2L flying-boats built by Boeing.*

Right: *Model 6 (B–1) in final form with 400hp Liberty engine and close-mounted wing floats.*

powered by a 300hp Wasp Junior pusher engine giving it a top speed of 122mph with a 4,000lb gross weight. Other variations from the C–204 included a metal (Alclad) hull skin, steel wing ribs and provision for fitting skis to permit operation from snow- and ice-covered areas. Only one example of the Totem was completed.

Above: *Model C–204 Thunderbird (CF–ALA) built by Boeing-Canada.* Below: *The sole Canadian-designed Totem, based on the Model C–204.* [Peter M. Bowers collection

Specification

SPAN	(B–1)	50ft 3in
	(Model 204)	39ft 8¼in
LENGTH	(B–1)	31ft 3in
	(Model 204)	32ft 7in
HEIGHT	(B–1)	13ft 4in
	(Model 204)	12ft 0in
WING AREA	(B–1)	492sq ft
	(Model 204)	470sq ft
GROSS WEIGHT	(B–1)	3,850lb
	(Model 204)	4,940lb
MAX SPEED	(B–1)	90mph
	(Model 204)	115mph
CRUISING SPEED	(B–1)	80mph
	(Model 204)	95mph
RANGE	(B–1)	400 miles
	(Model 204)	350 miles

Production

B–1	G–CADS
Model 6D (B–1D)	NC–5270
	G–CASX
Model 6E (B–1E)	NC–115E to NC–116E
	G–CATY
	G–CAUF
	CF–ABA to CF–ABB
Model 204	NC–874E
	NC–876E
Model 204A	NC–875E
Model C–204	CF–ALA to CF–ALD
Totem	CF–ARF

BB–1
(Model 7)

IN 1920 the Aircraft Manufacturing Co. of Vancouver purchased from Boeing the sole example of the BB–1. Like its immediate predecessor, this was a three-seat pusher flying-boat, though somewhat smaller overall than the B–1 and powered by a 130hp Hall-Scott L–4 engine. The wings had only a single bay of bracing struts each side, these being inclined inward slightly from the base and combining with those supporting the overhanging extremities of the upper wings to present an 'off-balance' V shape in frontal aspect. The upper as well as the lower wings were contoured to give an unbroken duo-curved shape at the tips, and (unlike the B–1) were unstaggered. A single cockpit aperture embraced all three occupants, the two passengers being seated side-by-side behind the pilot. First flight of the BB–1 was made on January 7, 1920.

Specification

SPAN	45ft 6in
LENGTH	27ft 8in
HEIGHT	11ft 8in
WING AREA	403sq ft
GROSS WEIGHT	2,699lb
MAX SPEED	84mph
CRUISING SPEED	75mph
RANGE	500 miles

Production
One (no registration)

Top: *Model 7 (BB–1).*

Right: *Model 8 (BB–L6).*

BB–L6
(Model 8)

THE MODEL 8 was another 'one-off' civil product, again reflecting the difficulty of competing with new (and therefore expensive) commercial designs in a market flooded with cut-price war-surplus military aeroplanes. The designation—implying a combination of the BB–1 wing design with the 200hp Hall-Scott L–6 engine—seems a curiously 'lazy' one, for in all other respects the aircraft was quite different from its predecessor. In the first place it was a landplane, and the fuselage was of completely different design with the engine installed and neatly cowled in the nose to drive a tractor propeller instead of the between-wing pusher installation of the flying-boat. Design of the plywood-covered fuselage is said to have been based upon that of the Italian Ansaldo Scout, an

example of which was available locally at the time. Seating arrangement was in two tandem cockpits, the pilot occupying the rear one with the two passengers seated side-by-side in front.

Built for Herb Munter, the Boeing Airplane Company's first professional test pilot, the BB–L6 was flown for the first time at Seattle on May 24, 1920, and was destroyed in a fire three years later. It is claimed to be the first aircraft to have flown over the nearby 14,400ft Mount Rainier, which has subsequently become a familiar backdrop for photographs of almost every other Boeing product.

Specification

SPAN	27ft 8in
LENGTH	29ft 3in
HEIGHT	10ft 10in
WING AREA	465sq ft
GROSS WEIGHT	2,632lb
MAX SPEED	100mph
CRUISING SPEED	90mph
RANGE	450 miles

Production
One (no registration)

GA–1
(Model 10)

THE GA–1 was one of two types built for the ground attack rôle by Boeing in 1921. The aircraft was designed, not by Boeing, but by I. M. Laddon for the US Army Air Service's Engineering Division, after AEF experience in 1918 had suggested the value of a heavily-armoured aircraft capable of flying slowly over enemy ground forces and bringing a heavy weight of firepower to bear on them. It was an angular, unstaggered triplane with two 435hp Liberty 12A engines driving pusher propellers and hav-

ing a multiplicity of N-pattern interplane bracing struts. It was heavily armour-plated around the crew stations and power plant, the remainder of the airframe being plywood- or fabric-covered.

The front section of each engine nacelle completely enclosed a gunner, whose only outlook was through shutters openable for the sighting of his two 0·30in machine-guns. Similar shutters were provided for the pilot. A nose gunner controlled the firing of an additional 0·30in gun rearward over the top wing, and that of a 37mm cannon also mounted in the nose; while a fourth gunner had one upward- and two down-

Boeing GA–X (said by some to indicate 'Guns, Armor and the Unknown Quantity') or GA–1, an unsuccessful ground attack design of 1921.

ward-firing machine-guns in the rear fuselage.

The prototype, known as the GA–X (Ground Attack—Experimental), was built by the Air Service Engineering Division at McCook Field, Ohio. A contract for 20 production GA–1s (later reduced to 10 after service trials in Texas) was awarded to Boeing, and the first of these was flown in May 1921. Although the entire batch was accepted by the Army, the GA–1 suffered from a number of aerodynamic deficiencies and power plant problems, and from the excessive weight of its 1-ton, ¼in-thick armour plating.

Specification

SPAN	65ft 6in
LENGTH	33ft 7in
HEIGHT	14ft 3in
WING AREA	1,016sq ft
GROSS WEIGHT	10,426lb
MAX SPEED	105mph
CRUISING SPEED	95mph
RANGE	350 miles

Production
64146–64155

GA–2
(Model 10)

ALTHOUGH ASSIGNED—retrospectively and purely for record purposes—the same Boeing Model number as the GA–1, the GA–2 bore no similarity to the GA–1 except in its intended rôle of ground attack. It, too, was designed by the Engineering Division of the USAAS, as was the single 750hp W–18 engine that powered it. The GA–2 was a two-bay biplane with equal-span wings, braced by parallel pairs of I-struts, and a short-legged main landing gear. It was heavily armour-plated, resulting in a gross weight less than a ton lighter than that of the GA–1. Accommodation was for a pilot and two gunners, who were responsible for a total armament of one 37mm and six 0·30in machine-guns.

Two GA–2 prototypes were built, both by Boeing, the second incorporating even more detail improvements than the first over the original Engineering Division design. Flight testing was undertaken entirely by the Army, but no production order was placed.

Specification

SPAN	54ft 0in
LENGTH	36ft 9in
HEIGHT	12ft 0in
WING AREA	851sq ft
GROSS WEIGHT	8,691lb
MAX SPEED	113mph
CRUISING SPEED	100mph
RANGE	200 miles

Production
64235–64236

The equally ugly—and equally unsuccessful—GA-2 design, given the same Boeing Model number (10) as the GA-1.

Thomas-Morse MB–3A

IN THE SPRING of 1918 the Thomas-Morse Aircraft Corporation of Ithaca, New York, was invited to design a new single-seat fighter with a performance superior to that of the French Spad fighters then being flown by AEF pursuit squadrons in Europe. The result was the MB–3, of which four prototypes were ordered; but the first of these did not fly until 1919. Nevertheless, the US Army placed an order with the parent company for 50 production MB–3s.

When, in 1920, tenders were invited for the manufacture of a further 200 similar aircraft, the contract was awarded to Boeing as the lowest bidder. These aircraft, designated MB–3A (no Boeing number was allotted), differed from the original MB–3 chiefly in the cooling system for the 320hp Wright H–3 engine, twin side-radiators mounted on the fuselage being found more efficient than the original

single radiator mounted in the upper wing centre-section. The radiators for the Boeing MB–3As were, however, manufactured by Thomas-Morse. On the final 50 fighters, Boeing also introduced modified, larger-area tail surfaces of its own design. Following several years in service with the Army Air Service, many of the MB–3As continued in use as advanced trainers, some until 1927.

Specification
SPAN	26ft 0in
LENGTH	20ft 0in
HEIGHT	7ft 8in
WING AREA	228sq ft
GROSS WEIGHT	2,539lb
MAX SPEED	140mph
CRUISING SPEED	125mph
ENDURANCE	$2\frac{1}{4}$hr

Production
68237 to 68436

PW–9/FB series
(Models 15, 53, 54, 55 and 67)

THE MODEL 15, initiated as a private venture, was Boeing's first attempt at designing a single-seat fighter, though conceived during the period when the company was contract-building the Thomas-Morse MB–3A fighter. The American Expeditionary Force, during 1917–18, had been equipped largely with combat aircraft of French origin, and the replacement of these by nationally-designed types seemed to offer a potentially promising market. The Model 15 prototype, following its first flight on June 2, 1923, was evaluated by the Army Air Service at McCook Field, and on September 9 that year Boeing was awarded a contract for two service prototypes. These were designated XPW–9 (Experimental Pursuit, Water-cooled engine). Just over a year later, on September 19, 1924, the AAS placed a production order for 12 PW–9s, increasing the figure to 30 at the end of the year. One additional aircraft was built for the NACA for research purposes.

Apart from the use of a divided-axle main landing gear the PW–9 was essentially similar to the prototype aircraft, having tapered biplane wings and a steel-tube fuselage (inspired by the example of the Fokker D.VII), and an armament of two

Left: *One of the final 50 Thomas-Morse MB–3As, which had Boeing-redesigned tail surfaces.*

Above right: *Original Boeing Model 15, photographed a month before its first flight. It was later given the designation XPW–9.*

Right: *First production PW–9C fighter.*

machine-guns in the upper front fuselage. In October 1925, delivery of the first PW-9s to units in Hawaii and the Philippines was accompanied by a further order, this time for 25 of a slightly modified version with duplicated landing wires, known as the PW-9A (Boeing Model 15A). Detail refinements to the landing and flying wires, and the landing gear, were incorporated in the 40 PW-9Cs (Model 15C), ordered in 1926 and including 15 aircraft originally begun as PW-9Bs. In August 1927, after conversion of the last PW-9C to serve as a prototype, the Army ordered a final batch of 16, designated PW-9D (Model 15D) and incorporating an aerodynamic-ally-balanced rudder and redesign of such features as the wheel brakes, engine cowling and radiator. The larger-area rudder, tested originally on the FB-3 (see p. 29), was fitted retrospectively to earlier models in the PW-9/FB series. Standard power plant of the PW-9/FB series was the 435hp Curtiss D-12 Vee-type engine.

Production of the Model 15 was also undertaken for the US Navy, beginning in 1925 with an order for 16 shore-based aircraft designated FB-1. Only 10 of these were built as FB-1s. They were basically similar to the PW-9, and were delivered initially to Marine Corps Squadrons 1, 2 and 3; later, they saw service with the USMC in China. Twenty-seven examples were completed of the FB-5 (Boeing Model 67), a version with a 520hp Packard 2A-1500 engine, increased wing stagger and balanced rudder. First flight of an FB-5 was made on October 7, 1926, and delivery of this batch was completed in January 1927 to USN Squadrons VF-1B and VF-6B aboard the USS *Langley*.

23

Experimental variants included one PW-9 fitted with wings built by Thomas-Morse having a corrugated metal upper skin; and others (described separately) which received the new designations XP-4, XP-7, XP-8 and AT-3. The remaining six aircraft of the Navy's FB-1 order were completed as experimental machines. Two became FB-2s (Boeing Model 53: FB-1s fitted with deck arrester gear for trials aboard the USS *Langley*); three FB-3s (Boeing Model 55) powered by 510hp Packard 1A-1500 engines and flown both with floats and with a split-axle wheel gear; and one FB-4 (Boeing Model 54), with a 450hp Wright P-1 radial engine and provision for floats. The FB-4, when refitted later with a 400hp Pratt & Whitney R-1340 Wasp radial, was redesignated FB-6; its Wasp installation provided the link with Boeing's next Navy fighter, the F2B, described separately.

Specification

SPAN	(PW-9C)	32ft 0in
	(FB-1)	32ft 0in
LENGTH	(PW-9C)	23ft 5in
	(FB-1)	23ft 5in
HEIGHT	(PW-9C)	8ft 2in
	(FB-1)	8ft 2in
WING AREA	(PW-9C)	260sq ft
	(FB-1)	260sq ft
GROSS WEIGHT	(PW-9C)	3,170lb
	(FB-1)	2,835lb
MAX SPEED	(PW-9C)	163mph
	(FB-1)	159mph
CRUISING SPEED	(PW-9C)	142mph
	(FB-1)	142mph
RANGE	(PW-9C)	390 miles
	(FB-1)	390 miles

Production

XPW–9 (Model 15)	23–1216 to 23–1218
PW–9	25–295 to 25–324
	One unregistered
	(for NACA)
PW–9A	26–351 to 26–373
PW–9B	26–375 (ordered as,
	and reverted to,
	PW–9A)
PW–9C	26–443 to 26–457
	27–178 to 27–202
PW–9D	27–202 (cvtd from
	PW–9C)
	28–26 to 28–41
FB–1	A–6884 to A–6893
FB–2	A–6894 to A–6895
FB–3	A–6897
	A–7089 to A–7090
FB–4	A–6896
FB–5	A–7101 to A–7127
FB–6	A–6896 (cvtd from
	FB–4

Above left: *FB–1 of Marine Corps Fighter Squadron VMF–6, San Diego.*

Left: *Second FB–3 (Model 55), with twin-float landing gear.*

Above right: *FB–4 (Model 54), with radial engine and float gear.*

Right: *FB–5 (Model 67), first production aircraft with the balanced rudder later adopted as standard for this version.*

DH–4/O2B series and XCO–7

(Models 16 and 42)

THE DE HAVILLAND D.H.4 two-seat day bomber, first flown in August 1916, was one of the best aircraft in its class during World War I. Seven British manufacturers built a total of 1,449, but an even greater number was built in the United States. In July 1917 a pattern aircraft was delivered to the US where, after refitting with a 400hp Liberty 12 engine, it made its first flight with this power plant on October 29, 1917. Plans were made for the production of these 'Liberty Planes' (designated DH–4) on a then-unprecedented scale involving the manufacture of well over 12,000 examples; even with the inevitable curtailment of this programme after the Armistice, the total number completed was 4,846. They were built by Dayton-Wright (3,106), the Fisher Body Division of General Motors (1,600) and Standard Aircraft Corporation (140). During and after the war, 283 DH–4s were transferred to the US Navy and Marine Corps. Only about 30 per cent of the total built had reached France before the war ended, but these served with 13 AEF squadrons (from August 1918) and four squadrons of the USN/USMC Northern Bombing Group.

The DH–4 came in for more than its fair share of criticism in the US: not only was it semi-obsolete by the late summer of 1918, but a considerable amount of re-design was needed to suit it to prevailing US methods of production. One major improvement made at an early stage (following British example in the D.H.9) was to transpose the locations of the front cockpit and main fuel tank, thus simultaneously improving crew intercommunication in flight and reducing the vulnerability of the fuel system. With this modification the aircraft received the designation DH–4B, and up to 1926 a total of 1,538 DH–4s were converted to this standard for both military and civil duties, including 111 by Boeing.

The next basic American development appeared in 1923, as the DH–4M (for Modernised). It still retained the Liberty 12A as the standard power plant, but the fuselage was of welded steel-tube construction, with fabric instead of plywood covering. Contracts were placed with Boeing in 1923 which resulted in the production of three XDH–4M–1 prototypes (later brought up to production standard), 147 DH–4M–1 aircraft for the US Army, and 30 basically similar machines for the Marine Corps designated O2B–1. Twenty-two of the DH–4M–1s were later converted to DH–4M–1T dual-control trainers. A further 135 similar DH–4M–2s were built by the Fokker-owned Atlantic Aircraft Corporation. Four of the Boeing O2B–1s, with improvements made by the Navy, were redesignated O2B–2, and one additional DH–4M–1 was completed for civil use as a mail-carrier. The DH–4B and DH–4M variants continued in first-line service with US Army and Marine Corps bomber and observation squadrons until 1928; they were then relegated to communications or training duties until withdrawn in 1932.

Under the new Boeing Model number 42, three of the DH–4M–1s were modified early in 1925 and given the Army designations XCO–7, –7A and –7B, signifying Experimental Corps Observation. They all had tapered, unequal-span wings, re-

Model 16 (XDH–4M–1), second of three rebuilt by Boeing with steel-tube fuselages.

26

designed tailplanes and a divided-Vee sprung landing gear. The first aircraft was for static testing only, while the third introduced an inverted engine installation and balanced elevators, but performance was not sufficiently improved to result in a production order.

Specification

SPAN	(DH–4B)	42ft 5in	
	(XCO–7A)	45ft 0in	
LENGTH	(DH–4B)	29ft 11in	
	(XCO–7A)	29ft 2in	
HEIGHT	(DH–4B)	9ft 8in	
	(XCO–7A)	10ft 8in	
WING AREA	(DH–4B)	440sq ft	
	(XCO–7A)	440sq ft	
GROSS WEIGHT	(DH–4B)	4,595lb	
	(XCO–7A)	4,665lb	
MAX SPEED	(DH–4B)	118mph	
	(XCO–7A)	122mph	
CRUISING SPEED	(DH–4B)	104mph	
	(XCO–7A)	110mph	
RANGE	(DH–4B)	330 miles	
	(XCO–7A)	420 miles	

Production

DH–4B	63461 to 63507
	63936
	63761 to 63823
	22–1000 to 22–1049
	Six for Cuba
DH–4 Mail	489 (civil)
XDH–4M–1	68590 to 68592
DH–4M–1	147 aircraft, random US Army serial numbers
O2B–1	A–6898 to A–6923
O2B–2	A–6924 to A–6927
XCO–7	22884
XCO–7A	23109
XCO–7B	31216

Above: *DH–4M–1 (O2B–1) of the US Marine Corps' 1st Aviation Group, 3rd Squadron.*

Below: *The XCO–7B, conversion of the DH–4M–1 with inverted Liberty engine, photographed in September 1924.*

NB–1 and NB–2
(Model 21)

FOLLOWING the Model 15 fighter, the next aircraft of Boeing design to go into production was the Model 21, a two-seat unstaggered biplane evolved as a primary trainer for the US Navy and capable of operation on either a wheeled or a single-float landing gear. The prototype was tested under the somewhat inaccurate Navy designation VNB–1 (the V simply indicating a heavier-than-air design), but in its original form was too easy to fly and incapable of being spun. Initial modifications made to overcome this defect in the 41 production NB–1s erred dangerously in the opposite direction, but eventually a satisfactory compromise was reached and the design was accepted. Various J-series Wright radial engines were installed in these aircraft, which were followed by a batch of 30, designated NB–2, in which the power plant was the 180hp Wright-built Hispano-Suiza E–4 Vee-type engine. Boeing also built and delivered five Model 21s, with Lawrance engines, to the government of Peru.

The NB–1 and –2 were employed both for pilot training and, with a 0·30in machine-gun on a Scarff ring in the rear cockpit, for gunnery training; many were still in service at the end of 1927. A third use for the type was also found by the Marine Corps, which in 1929 modified a number of NB–1s to carry out anti-mosquito crop-spraying work in Puerto Rico. The USN used one NB–1 in 1925 to test a new type of oleo shock-absorber. Two others, redesignated NB–3 and NB–4, were used for further series of spinning tests in 1925 but later restored to NB–1 standard.

Specification

SPAN	36ft 10in
LENGTH	(seaplane) 28ft 9in
HEIGHT	11ft 7in
WING AREA	344sq ft
GROSS WEIGHT	(NB–1) 2,837lb
	(NB–2) 3,037lb
MAX SPEED	99·5mph
CRUISING SPEED	90mph
RANGE	300 miles

Production

VNB–1	A–6749
Model 21	Five for Peru
NB–1	A–6750 to A–6768
	A–6836 to A–6857
NB–2	A–6769 to A–6798
NB–3	A–6856 (cvtd from NB–1)
NB–4	A–6857 (cvtd from NB–1)

Left: *US Navy NB–1 gunnery trainer with land-plane undercarriage.* [US Navy

Above right: *Liberty-engined original Model 40 prototype.*

Right: *Model 40A in the San Francisco–Chicago 'Bee-line' insignia of Boeing Air Transport, 1927.*

Model 40

In 1925 the US Post Office Department held a design competition to find a replacement for the DH–4 which had been its standard mail-carrying aeroplane since 1918. The specification stipulated use of the Liberty engine, and Boeing's entry, the Model 40, flew for the first time on July 7, 1925. It was an elegant biplane whose mixed-construction fuselage of wood and steel tube was smoothly contoured and covered for most of its length with wood veneer. The Post Office, although buying the prototype, did not place a production order, and since it was the only possible customer for the aircraft Boeing temporarily discontinued development of the design. (The Model 40 was the first Boeing design to receive a Model number from the outset; numbers 1–39 were then applied in retrospect to earlier designs.)

Late the following year, however, it was learned that trans-continental air mail routes in the US were to be handed over to private operators from July 1927; applications were to be heard in January. Boeing therefore revived the Model 40, redesigning and improving it to meet the latest requirements. With its fabric-covered steel-tube fuselage and uncowled 420hp Wasp radial engine, the redesigned Model 40A may have been less handsome than its progenitor, but it did have a much-improved payload/performance spectrum. Moreover, with a two-seat passenger cabin installed just aft of the forward mail compartment, it was not dependent upon mail alone to provide the payload. Post Office acceptance of Boeing's bid for the San Francisco–Chicago mail route enabled the company to initiate production of 25 Model 40As—only the second design to receive an Approved Type Certificate under new Department of Commerce regulations introduced in January 1927—and to form a new company, Boeing Air Transport Inc, to operate the service. The first production 40A was flown on June 29, 1927, and delivery of 24 was completed two days before the new service was due to open on July 1. The 25th aircraft was delivered to Pratt & Whitney as an engine testbed, and when the new 525hp Hornet radial became available in early 1928 the 40As were re-equipped with these engines and redesignated Model 40B. Two 40Bs were further modified to have two cockpits in tandem and dual controls.

The Hornet engine also powered the next production version, which seated four passengers internally and introduced various detail improvements, both external and internal. This was designated Model 40B–4 (the two-passenger version becoming 40B–2 in retrospect), and the first example was flown on October 5, 1929. By the time production ended early in 1932 a total of 38 had been built, for customers who included United Air Lines, Western Airlines, Western Canada Airways and Pacific Air Transport. A 39th machine was built as an engine test vehicle for Pratt &

Whitney, and Boeing-Canada completed four others designated as Model 40H–4. A fifth 40H–4 was not completed.

The 40B–4 was preceded, despite the later designation, by 10 examples of a Wasp-engined four-passenger version known as the Model 40C. Nine of these were to an order from Pacific Air Transport: this operator was absorbed into Boeing Air Transport late in 1928, the joint concern then being renamed The Boeing System. With the exception of one PAT aircraft, all were in due course converted to 40B–4 standard, but during 1928 two 'one-off' modified 40Cs were delivered, one to Associated Oil and one to Standard Oil. Designated Models 40X and 40Y respectively, each was a two-passenger, two-crew machine, the former powered by a Wasp engine and the latter by a Hornet.

Specification

SPAN	44ft 2¼in
LENGTH	33ft 2¼in
HEIGHT	12ft 3⅛in
WING AREA	547sq ft
GROSS WEIGHT	(Model 40A) 6,000lb
	(Model 40B–4) 6,075lb
MAX SPEED	(Model 40A) 128mph
	(Model 40B–4) 137mph
CRUISING SPEED	(Model 40A) 105mph
	(Model 40B–4) 125mph
RANGE	(Model 40A) 650 miles
	(Model 40B–4) 535 miles

Model 40B–4 (converted from 40C) of United Air Lines in the early 1930s.

30

Production

Model 40	Prototype, no registration
Model 40A	C–268 to C–292
Model 40B–4	C–278K
	C–740K to C–743K
	NC–830M to NC–837M
	CF–AIM to CF–AIO
	NC–842M to NC–843M
	NC–10338 to NC–10357
Model 40B–4A	X–813M
Model 40C	C–6841
	C–5389 to C–5390
	C–5339 to C–5340
	C–178E to C–181E
	NC–841M
Model 40H–4	CF–AMP to CF–AMT
Model 40X	NC–7526
Model 40Y	NC–381

PB–1
(Model 50)

CONSIDERABLE ATTENTION was paid by both the US Army and Navy during the 1920s to the fostering of long-distance flying, as exemplified by the Army's Douglas World Cruiser flights of 1924. A suitable yardstick for long-distance flights by Navy aircraft was the 2,000 miles or more between the western US seaboard and Hawaii, and in 1924 the USN issued a specification for a twin-engined patrol flying-boat capable of completing such a journey non-stop. To meet this, Boeing built the Navy-designed PB–1 as its Model 50, in which the two 800hp Packard 2A–2500 engines were mounted back-to-back, mid-way between

the wings, on the aircraft centre-line, to drive one tractor and one pusher propeller. Apart from the engine arrangement the PB–1 was conventional in appearance, though a number of novel features were revealed in its construction. These included the use of tubular metal for the wing spars and ribs, metal for the lower half of the two-step hull and wood for the upper half. Wide-span ailerons (there were no flaps) were supplemented by auxiliary aerofoil surfaces above the upper pair.

The sole PB–1 was completed in 1925, but did not make the proposed non-stop San Francisco–Hawaii flight after the feat was accomplished instead by the Naval Aircraft Factory's own PN–9 flying-boat in September 1925. It remained in Navy service, however, and in 1928 was refitted by the NAF with experimental geared Pratt & Whitney Hornet radial engines (also of 800hp each) and redesignated XPB–2.

Specification

SPAN	87ft 6in
LENGTH	59ft 4½in
HEIGHT	20ft 10¼in
WING AREA	1,801sq ft
GROSS WEIGHT	26,822lb
MAX SPEED	112mph
CRUISING SPEED	94mph
RANGE	2,500 miles

Production
A–6881

XP–4
(Model 58)

IN 1924 the US Army Air Service adopted a simplified designation system for its aircraft in which the former PW (Pursuit, Water-cooled engine) and other fighter prefix groups were replaced by the single prefix letter P. The Boeing PW–9 in fact retained its original designation throughout its service life, but a number of PW–9 variants, modified sufficiently to justify a new designation, were numbered under the new system.

The first of these, the XP–4, was actually the last of the 30 PW–9s ordered by the Army, modified as an experimental high-altitude fighter. To this end the 510hp Packard 1A–1500 engine was fitted with a turbo-supercharger and a large, four-blade propeller, and the wing area was increased by 49sq ft by extending the span of the lower wings to match that of the upper ones. The aerofoil section of both wings

Top: *PB–1 (Model 50) flying-boat with original Packard engines.*

Left: *XP–4 (Model 58).* [USAF

31

was also changed, and the two machine-guns moved to a new location in the lower wings, outboard of the propeller arc. The aircraft was delivered to the Army in July 1926. However, the increased wing area was insufficient to compensate for the added weight—cruising speed was actually 5mph slower than the PW–9—and no production contract for the XP–4 was placed.

Specification

SPAN	32ft 0in
LENGTH	23ft 11in
HEIGHT	8ft 10in
WING AREA	309sq ft
GROSS WEIGHT	3,650lb
MAX SPEED	161mph
CRUISING SPEED	137mph
RANGE	375 miles

Production
25–324 (cvtd from PW–9)

The XTB–1, first of three Model 63 torpedo float-planes, photographed in 1927.

TB–1
(Model 63)

THE TB–1 was a three-seat torpedo-carrying biplane designed by the US Navy in 1927 and capable of operating either from aircraft carriers (with a four-wheel landing gear) or as a twin-float seaplane. In either form the landing gear was divided to allow the suspension of a 1,740lb torpedo beneath the centre of the fuselage. The front cockpit, just forward of the wings, seated a pilot and a navigator/bombardier side-by-side; the rear gunner's cockpit was situated mid-way between the wings and the tail unit. Power plant was a 730hp Packard 3A–2500 Vee-type engine. Basically, the TB–1 was a development of the Navy/Martin T3M torpedo aircraft, with a fabric-covered all-metal airframe, and the wings could be folded back for storage on board ship.

Construction of three aircraft was allocated to Boeing. The XTB–1 prototype flew for the first time on May 4, 1927, and all three were delivered by mid-year. No further examples were built, the Navy having decided by then to specify a twin-engined aircraft to carry out this particular rôle. For Boeing, the TB–1 represented the last non-company-designed type, with the exception of the Blackburn Sharks built by Boeing-Canada in 1937, to be manufactured prior to World War II.

Specification

SPAN	55ft 0in
LENGTH	40ft 10in
HEIGHT	13ft 6in
WING AREA	868sq ft
GROSS WEIGHT	9,786lb
MAX SPEED	115mph
CRUISING SPEED	100mph
RANGE	878 miles

Production
A–7024 to A–7026

Model 64

BUILT AS a private venture, the Boeing Model 64 was a two-seat, staggered biplane designed as a primary or gunnery trainer to replace the NB series. Variations were made in the wing section and interplane bracing, in an endeavour to eliminate the spinning difficulties encountered in the earlier type, and the prototype made its first flight—as a two-bay machine with thin-section wings—in February 1926. Provision existed for a synchronised front-mounted machine-gun, with a second, movable gun on a ring mounting in the rear cockpit.

Although submitted to both the Navy and Army, the Model 64 was accepted by neither, and consequently no service designation was allotted. The prototype was eventually sold to Pacific Air Transport, who in turn replaced the original 200hp Wright J-3 radial engine with a 220hp Wright J-5 and resold it to a private customer. Work on a second machine was begun, but it is uncertain whether this was completed.

Specification

SPAN	36ft 10in
LENGTH	25ft 4½in
HEIGHT	11ft 1in
WING AREA	344sq ft
GROSS WEIGHT	2,840lb
MAX SPEED	99mph
CRUISING SPEED	84mph
RANGE	250 miles

Production
N7268

Original thin-winged Model 64 in March 1926.

XP–8
(Model 66)

ALTHOUGH NATURALLY drawing extensively upon the design and constructional features of the PW–9/FB series of fighters, the Model 66 was essentially a completely new concept. It was evolved in 1925 to meet an Army Air Service requirement, issued in April of that year, for a single-seat fighter designed around the new 600hp Packard 2A–1500 inverted-Vee engine. The most notable feature in the XP–8's design was the location of the cooling radiator, between the underside of the fuselage and the lower wing centre-section. The Army supplied the engine and military equipment, but did not officially purchase the aircraft from Boeing until the beginning of 1928, although it had taken delivery of it for testing in July 1927. Although it was scrapped in mid-1929 without a production order being placed, the XP–8 provided a number of design features that were incorporated in the F2B–1 Navy fighter and other later Boeing products.

Specification

SPAN	30ft 1in
LENGTH	22ft 10in
HEIGHT	10ft 9in
WING AREA	242sq ft
GROSS WEIGHT	3,421lb
MAX SPEED	173mph
CRUISING SPEED	148mph
RANGE	325 miles

Production
28–359

AT-3
(Model 68)

THE AT–3 was a 'one-off' conversion, at Army Air Corps request, of a PW–9A fighter to single-seat advanced trainer configuration. The conversion consisted basically of reworking the airframe of the penultimate PW–9A to accept a 180hp Wright-Hispano engine in place of the standard 435hp Curtiss D–12. Since the structure was in no way restressed or rebuilt commensurate with its new power/ weight ratio the performance of the AT–3 was predictably disappointing and it was not ordered into production.

Specification

SPAN	32ft 0in
LENGTH	23ft 5in
HEIGHT	8ft 2in
WING AREA	260sq ft
GROSS WEIGHT	2,648lb
MAX SPEED	129mph

Production
26–374 (cvtd from PW–9A)

Top: *Model 66 (XP–8), with radiator mounted in the lower wing root.* [USAF

Left: *Model 68 (AT–3) converted as an experimental trainer from a PW–9A fighter in 1926.*

F2B-1
(Model 69)

INSTALLATION OF THE Pratt & Whitney Wasp radial engine in the experimental FB–6 has already been described. This installation, in the form of a 425hp R–1340, was retained virtually unaltered in Boeing's next Navy fighter, a private-venture project which was allocated the company Model number 69. The prototype, designated XF2B–1, flew for the first time on November 3, 1926, the propeller being fitted with a flat parabolic spinner rather like that of the earlier FB–4. This refinement was omitted from the 32 production F2B–1s which were ordered following testing of the prototype fighter during 1927, and the original non-balanced rudder was replaced by a balanced one.

Notwithstanding its fighter designation, the F2B–1 was also equipped to carry five 25lb bombs under the lower wings and fuselage, and the production aircraft were assigned initially to fighter squadron VF–1B and bomber squadron VB–2B, both aboard the USS *Saratoga*; deliveries began in January 1928. It was the latter squadron which gave the US Navy its first aerobatic team, beginning with a trio of F2B–1s (known as 'the Three Sea Hawks') and eventually developing a formation display in which the entire squadron flew tied together throughout its performance. Two further machines, identified as Model 69–B, were built, one each for the Brazilian and Japanese governments.

Specification

SPAN	30ft 1in
LENGTH	22ft 11in
HEIGHT	9ft 2¾in
WING AREA	243sq ft
GROSS WEIGHT	2,805lb
MAX SPEED	158mph
CRUISING SPEED	132mph
RANGE	317 miles

Production

XF2B–1	A–7385
F2B–1	A–7424 to A–7455
Model 69–B	One for Brazil
	One for Japan

F3B-1
(Models 74 and 77)

PRIVATE-VENTURE DEVELOPMENT of its Navy fighter series was continued by Boeing with the Model 74, which was essentially an improved version of the Model 69. The XF3B–1 prototype, as first flown on March 2, 1927, and subsequently evaluated by the US Navy, was in essence an XF2B–1 airframe (minus the spinner) with an FB–5 landing gear and a 425hp R–1340 Wasp engine. In this form, and later with a centre-float landing gear, it showed only a slight performance increase over the F2B–1 and was, therefore, returned to the company for further development.

This took the form of lengthening the forward fuselage, completely redesigning the tail unit construction and the wheel landing gear, and fitting new sweptback, longer-span upper wings and non-swept lower wings, all of constant chord. A further change, in the contours of the vertical tail surfaces, was made in the F3B–1 production version. After the rebuilt prototype (renumbered as Model 77)

Sixth production F2B–1 in the colours of US Navy Squadron VF–6B, USS Langley.

had flown on February 3, 1928, deliveries of 73 F3B–1s were made between the following August-November. These, like the F2B–1s, were initially divided between Navy carrier-based fighter and bomber squadrons, as follows: VF–2B (*Langley*), VF–3B and VB–1B (*Lexington*), and VB–2B (*Saratoga*). They were largely withdrawn from these units by 1932, but continued to serve for some years in a staff or command transport capacity.

Specification

SPAN	33ft 0in
LENGTH	24ft 10in
HEIGHT	9ft 2in
WING AREA	275sq ft
GROSS WEIGHT	2,945lb
MAX SPEED	157mph
CRUISING SPEED	131mph
RANGE	340 miles

Production

XF3B–1	A–7674
F3B–1	A–7675 to A–7691
	A–7708 to A–7763

Top: *Model 74 (XF3B–1) in initial test form with landplane undercarriage.*

Left: *F3B–1 (Model 77) of Bomber Squadron VF–3B, USS* Lexington.

Above right: *Third Boeing Model 80 with drag rings on outer engines and modified vertical tail surfaces.*

Right: *Fourth Model 80A, with enlarged fuel tanks and still-further-modified tail contours.*

Models 80 and 226

THE AMOUNT OF BUSINESS done by Boeing Air Transport's two- and four-passenger single-engined Model 40s was sufficient to encourage Boeing to develop a larger aircraft designed expressly for passenger services. The result was the Model 80, of which the first of four examples flew for the first time early in August 1928. The Model 80 was a three-engined biplane, with the two outboard Wasp 410hp radial engines mounted mid-way between the upper and lower wings. Accommodation included a flight crew of two, a stewardess, 12 passengers in a three-abreast seating layout, and up to 1,000lb of cargo. The passenger cabin was ventilated, and amenities included leather-upholstered seats, individual reading lights and hot and cold running water. The stewardesses—the world's first—were registered nurses engaged by BAT to minister to the passengers' needs.

The original four aircraft were followed by ten examples of the Model 80A, an improved version distinguished by its 525hp Hornet engines, parallel wing bracing struts, larger upper-wing fuel tanks, and revised nose and fin and rudder shapes. In these aircraft the cargo capacity was marginally smaller, but the passenger capacity was increased to 18 and the cruising speed by 10mph. NACA engine cowlings were fitted at first, though removed when the 80A began airline operation; but cowling rings and the remodelled vertical tail design were applied retrospectively to the original four Model 80s. Later modifications to the BAT Model 80As included a reduction in fuel capacity and the addition of small auxiliary

37

fins and rudders at about two-thirds out along the tailplane span. In this form the aircraft were redesignated Model 80A-1; they were withdrawn from regular airline service in 1933 following the appearance of the Boeing Model 247. Boeing continued to use one 80A-1 at its School of Aeronautics at Oakland, California, and one other aircraft (NC–224M) eventually found its way to Alaska where, with a large cargo door installed in the starboard side of the rear fuselage, it was still busy transporting mining equipment and other heavy freight up to the end of World War II.

Two other aircraft, originally laid down as Model 80As, were actually completed to alternative configurations. One, designated Model 80B-1, was powered by Hornet engines and had a built-up nose with the crew seated above it in an elevated open cockpit that allowed them to see rearward over the upper wing. Later, when BAT pilots had been persuaded of the advantages of enclosed cockpits, this machine was converted to the 80A-1 configuration originally intended for it. The other machine (NC–233M), built for the Standard Oil Company of California, was considerably modified internally and received the new Model number 226. Delivered at the end of 1930, it had a six-seat executive interior, including two convertible beds, chairs and tables, a stove, sink and refrigerator. Externally, it could be distinguished by its larger cabin windows and (until they were removed in service) engine drag rings and large streamlined main wheel fairings.

Specification (Model 80A)

SPAN	80ft 0in
LENGTH	56ft 6in
HEIGHT	15ft 3in
WING AREA	1,220sq ft
GROSS WEIGHT	17,500lb
MAX SPEED	138mph
CRUISING SPEED	125mph
RANGE	460 miles

Production

Model 80	7135 to 7138
Model 80A	793K
	C–224M to C–232M
Model 80B	NC–234M
Model 226	NC–233M

Top: *Boeing 80A-1, operated by National Air Tours Inc of Seattle.*

Left: *Boeing Model 226, developed from the 80A as an executive aircraft for the Standard Oil Company in 1930.*

Right: *Model 81 (XN2B-1), with four-cylinder Fairchild-Caminez radial engine and four-blade propeller.*

Model 81
(XN2B-1)

IN ITS ORIGINAL FORM the Boeing Model 64 was fitted with thin-section wings, but trials were also made later using a thicker aerofoil section. From the latter design Boeing developed and built two examples of the Model 81, also intended as a primary trainer. Power plant for the Model 81 was a new-style radial engine, the four-cylinder Fairchild-Caminez, which produced 125hp for a much lower crankshaft speed than other contemporary radials of similar power. During tests using both two- and four-blade propellers this engine gave rise to a number of problems, and both aircraft were in due course refitted with more conventional power plants. The first, re-flown on December 27, 1928, with a 145hp Axelson radial, was then redesignated Model 81A and used at Boeing's Oakland (California) School of Aeronautics, where it underwent a further succession of engine changes. These included a 115hp Axelson

and 165hp Wright J-6-5 (Model 81B), and a 100hp Kinner K-5 with which, plus a new fin and rudder design, it became the Model 81C.

The second machine, evaluated by the US Navy as the XN2B-1 during the second half of 1928, was re-engined early in the following year with a 160hp Wright J-6-7. Performance with the latter engine was considerably better, but no production order for the aircraft was placed.

Specification

SPAN	35ft 0in
LENGTH	25ft 8in
HEIGHT	11ft 2in
WING AREA	295sq ft
GROSS WEIGHT	2,178lb
MAX SPEED	113mph
CRUISING SPEED	86mph
RANGE	335 miles

Production

Model 81A, B, C	X-63E
XN2B-1	A-8010

F4B/P-12 series
(Models 83, 89, 99, 100, 101, 102, 218, 222, 223, 227, 234, 235, 251, 256 and 267)

EARLY IN 1928 the biggest single success of Boeing's 12-year existence began with the appearance of two private-venture fighter prototypes, bearing the Boeing Model numbers 83 and 89. By the time that production came to an end five years later, nearly 600 aircraft in this fighter series had been built for the US services and other customers, and several were still in use when America entered World War II. The Boeing 83 and 89 prototypes were each powered by a 450hp Pratt & Whitney R-1340B Wasp radial engine; design and construction were conventional, based on a metal-framework fuselage and constant-chord fabric-covered wooden wings, and the two prototypes differed in detail only. First flights were made on June 25 and August 7, 1928, respectively, both aircraft subsequently undergoing evaluation by the US Navy and, in the case of the Model 89, the US Army.

Naval testing quickly resulted in an order for 27 production aircraft, designated F4B-1 (Boeing Model 99). These incorporated the deck arrester gear of the Boeing 83 with the Model 89's divided-axle landing gear and provision for an under-fuselage 500lb bomb, in addition to the standard facility for five 24lb bombs under each lower wing. To these were added the two prototype aircraft which, although sometimes described for clarity as XF4B-1s, were in fact modified in due course to full F4B-1 standard. The first production F4B-1 was flown on May 6, 1929. Deliv-

eries, to squadrons VB–1B (USS *Lexington*) and VF–2B (USS *Langley*), began some six weeks later and were completed in the following August. Various modifications were introduced during the F4B–1's service life, among them the addition of Townend engine cowling rings and the broad-chord fin surfaces introduced later on the F4B–4. The fourth production F4B–1, with armament deleted and redesignated F4B–1A, was allocated to the Assistant Secretary of the Navy as a staff aircraft.

A more modest initial order—for ten aircraft—was placed by the US Army Air Corps after testing the Model 89 at Bolling Field in mid-1928. Nine of these were completed as P–12s (Boeing Model 102), and were basically identical with the F4B–1 except for the absence of arrester hooks. The first P–12 was flown to Central America on a goodwill mission in February 1929 by Captain Ira C. Eaker; delivery to the Army of this and the other eight P–12s was completed in April.

The tenth aircraft (Boeing Model 101) differed in having non-tapered Frisetype ailerons, redesigned elevators, a shorter landing gear and a fully-cowled engine. Designated XP–12A, it made its first flight on April 11, 1929, but was unfortunately lost in a mid-air collision before its improved features could be fully assessed. Nevertheless the improved-style

Top: *Model 89, second of two prototypes for the P–12/F4B series, in July 1928.*

Right: *Boeing F4B–1 of Navy Squadron VF–5B, USS* Lexington.

ailerons and elevators were introduced on the P–12B fighter (Boeing Model 102B), of which 90 were ordered in June 1929 and delivered between February and May 1930. Further changes were evident in the next two Army models. In June 1930 the USAAC placed a contract for 131 P–12Cs (Boeing 222), to combine the P–12B airframe with a later, ring-cowled engine and a cross-axle landing gear with a spreader bar, similar to that of the original Model 83. In the event, only 96 of these were designated as P–12Cs, the remaining 35 being known as P–12Ds (Boeing Model 227) although outwardly identical. All 131 aircraft were delivered by the end of April 1931, P–12D units including the 35th and 36th Pursuit Squadrons. Prior to this, in 1930, the US Navy placed another order for 46 of the Boeing fighters. These, known as F4B–2s (Boeing Model 223), corresponded to the P–12C and incorporated the cross-axle landing gear, a wheel in place of a tailskid, a ring-cowled engine and Frise-type ailerons. They were delivered in January-May 1931, to VF–6B (USS *Saratoga*) and VF–5B (formerly VB–1B, USS *Lexington*). As with their predecessors, F4B–4 fin surfaces were later substituted for the original type. Standard armament, throughout the F4B/P–12 series, was a pair of 0·30in machine guns in the upper front fuselage.

Meanwhile, on September 29, 1930,

Top: *Third of nine P–12 (Model 102) fighters ordered by the US Army Air Corps.*

Right: *P–12B, with a P–12C-type cowling ring as fitted later to some aircraft.* [Gordon S. Williams

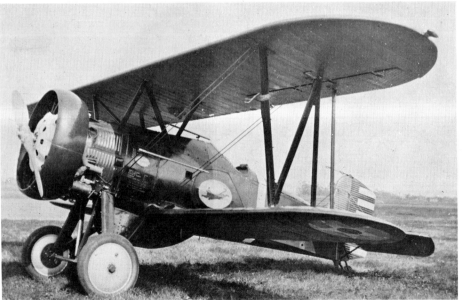

another significant prototype had made its first flight in the hands of a company pilot. Although having the outward appearance of the P–12B, in fact it marked a major structural advance, for it had a duralumin-skinned semi-monocoque fuselage very similar to those which the company had developed for the Models 96, 202 and 205. Similarity was enhanced soon after the first flight, when the fin and rudder contours were also changed to match those of the Models 202/205. Known by Boeing as the Model 218, the new prototype was tested with both R–1340D and R–1340E Wasp engines (Army designations XP–925 and XP–925A respectively) and with such other refinements as streamlined 'spat' fairings over the main wheels. In 1932, when its Boeing/Army test programme was over, the Model 218 was sold to China, where it was eventually shot down over Shanghai after accounting for two of the three Japanese fighters which had attacked it.

The immediate outcome of the Boeing 218 flight tests was an Army contract, in March 1931, for 135 P–12E fighters (Boeing Model 234), based on the P–12D but incorporating the all-metal fuselage and new tail contours. This represented Boeing's largest single military order since the MB–3A contract of 1921. Of this order, 110 aircraft were delivered as P–12Es (the

Top: *F4B–2, Naval equivalent to the P–12C with undercarriage spreader-bar, tail wheel and ring cowling.*

Left: *Boeing P–12D, with ventral auxiliary fuel tank.*

Right: *The metal-fuselage Model 218 prototype in November 1930, after adoption of restyled rudder.*

first example flying on October 15, 1931); recipients included the 27th Pursuit Squadron and the 95th Attack Squadron. The other 25 aircraft were delivered as P-12Fs (Boeing Model 251), with SR-1340G engines that gave them a better performance at altitude; the final P-12F was fitted experimentally with an enclosed cockpit. A month after the Army contract, the US Navy also placed orders for 113 production fighters based on the Model 218. These comprised 21 F4B-3s and 92 F4B-4s, both types carrying the Boeing Model number 235 and corresponding to the Army P-12E except for minor detail and equipment variations. The F4B-4, as already indicated, was distinguishable by its broader-chord fin, a feature later applied as a retrofit to the F4B-1s and F4B-2s in service. The first F4B-3s were delivered (to VF-1B, USS *Saratoga*) in December 1931, and the last F4B-4 in February 1933; of the latter, 21 were delivered to the Marine Corps (which also assembled a 22nd aircraft from spares), for service initially with Squadron VMF-10. The Navy F4B-4s served originally with VF-3B (USS *Langley*) and VF-6B (USS *Saratoga*). The final 45 aircraft on the F4B-4 order were each equipped with a life raft, housed in an enlarged headrest fairing behind the cockpit.

A number of P-12 series airframes were utilised for various experimental purposes, but were not allotted separate Boeing Model numbers. The XP-12G was a P-12B airframe (with a P-12C cowling ring) used to flight-test the YISR-1340G and H turbo-supercharged Wasp engines, after which it was restored to a P-12B. Another engine testbed was the XP-12H (experimental geared GISR-1340E), converted from and eventually restored to a P-12D. The XP-12E and P-12J were both converted from standard production P-12Es, the latter being fitted with a 575hp SR-1340H Wasp engine and a new-type bomb-sight. These two machines, and five other P-12Es, underwent further service trials as YP-12Ks when fitted with SR-1340E fuel-injection engines. All seven aircraft were restored to standard P-12Es in June 1938, but not before the XP-12E/YP-12K had undergone a three-year test period (1934–37) with an F-7 turbo-supercharger, during which it was designated XP-12L. In 1940 the US Army planned the conversion of one obsolete P-12E as an unmanned, radio-controlled target aircraft, designated A-5. This conversion was not carried out, but in 1941 a collection of 23 assorted P-12 series aircraft were handed over to the Navy for a similar purpose; they were given the Navy designation F4B-4A, the suffix letter in this case indicating their Army origin in accordance with standard designation procedure. Two genuine F4B-4s, both ex-USMC machines, were handed over in 1940 to the US Bureau of Air Commerce (forerunner of the FAA), which in turn sold them to private customers. One of these has since come into the collection of the Naval Aviation Museum at Pensacola, Florida; another machine, a P-12E, is

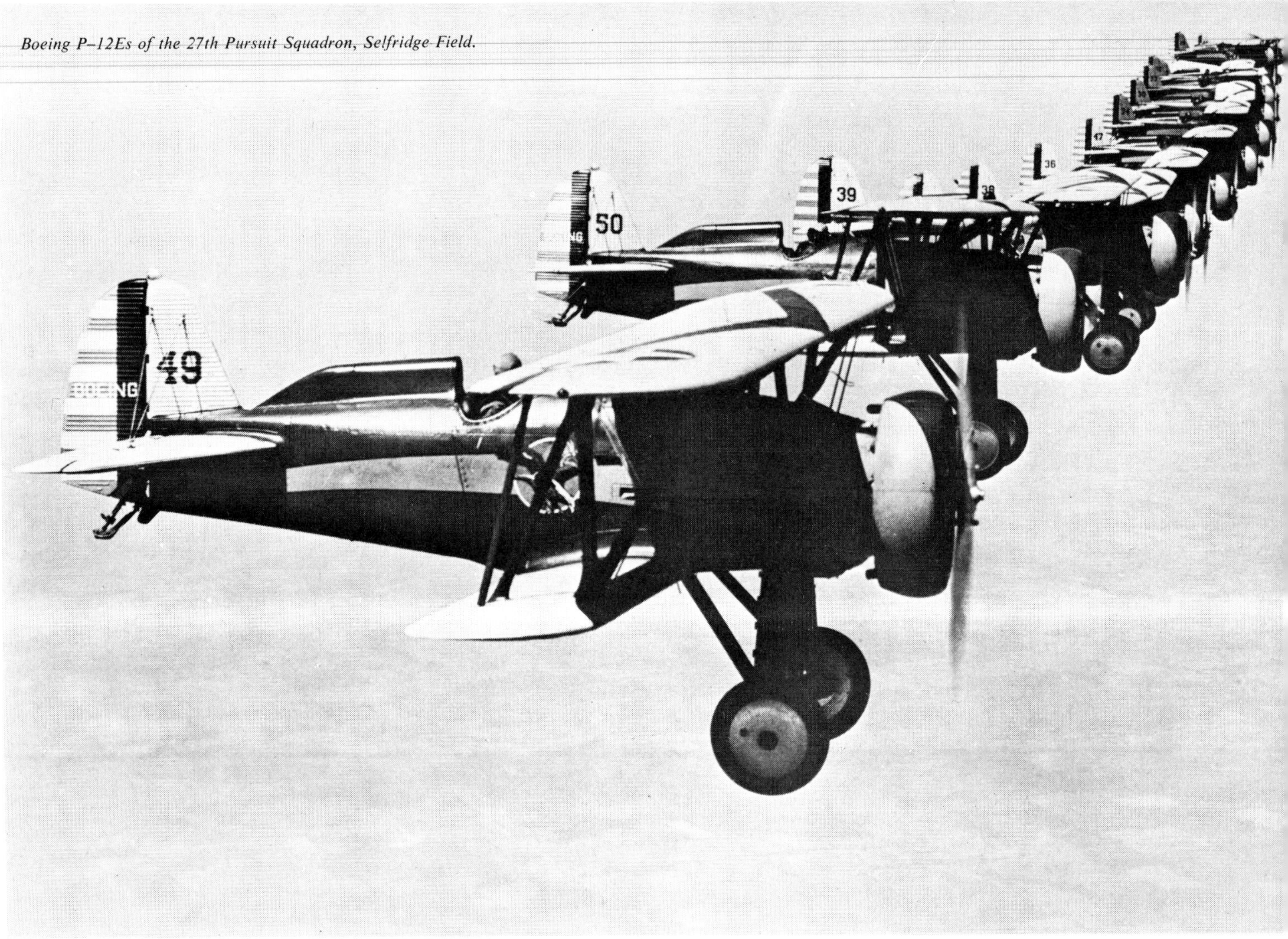

Boeing P–12Es of the 27th Pursuit Squadron, Selfridge Field.

P–12F, similar to the P–12E but with SR–1340G engine and better altitude performance.
[Peter M. Bowers collection

Second of 21 F4B–3s, prior to delivery to Navy Squadron VF–3B (USS Saratoga) in 1932–33.

maintained by the Air Museum at Ontario, California.

During the production life of the F4B/P–12 series, Boeing also manufactured a number of these aircraft for commercial or export sale. Four Model 100s, unarmed counterparts of the F4B–1, were built, of which the first was delivered to the Bureau of Air Commerce. Pratt & Whitney bought the second, using it as a test aircraft for various Wasp, Twin Wasp and Hornet engines. The other two, used at first as company demonstrators, were also sold later, one to the Boeing School of Aeronautics, which later sold it to Paul Mantz, and one to the Mitsui Co in Japan.

The Model 100s were preceded by one two-seat Model 100A, built for Howard Hughes, and followed by two Model 100Es (P–12Es) for Thailand. The Boeing 100F was a 'commercial' P–12F, bought by Pratt & Whitney for engine tests. In 1932, the first 14 aircraft of the US Navy's F4B–4 order were completed, with modifications, to meet a Brazilian Air Force order. These were delivered in the Autumn of 1932 as landplanes, without flotation gear, arrester hooks, radio and armament, and were designated Model 256. A follow-on order for a further nine aircraft was completed in February 1933. These had the Model number 267, differing from the Boeing 256 in having P–12E wings allied to the fuselage, tail assembly and landing gear of the F4B–3.

On February 28, 1933, a week after completing the second Brazilian order, Boeing delivered to the US Navy the final F4B–4, so bringing to an end an important era in the company's history. This series had represented the last biplane fighters to be manufactured by Boeing; were the last wooden-winged company designs to be built at Seattle; and made up the largest production total (586 aircraft, including prototypes) to be built by the company between the MB–3A contract of 1921 and the eve of World War II.

Specification

SPAN	(F4B–1)	30ft 0in
	(P–12E)	30ft 0in
LENGTH	(F4B–1)	20ft 1in
	(P–12E)	20ft 3in
HEIGHT	(F4B–1)	9ft 4in
	(P–12E)	9ft 0in
WING AREA		227·5sq ft
GROSS WEIGHT	(F4B–1)	2,750lb
	(P–12E)	2,690lb
MAX SPEED	(F4B–1)	176mph
	(P–12E)	189mph
CRUISING SPEED	(F4B–1)	150mph
	(P–12E)	160mph
RANGE	(F4B–1)	371 miles
	(P–12E)	520 miles

A Boeing F4B–4 with the green tail of Squadron VB–5, which served aboard both the Ranger *and the* Lexington *while equipped with these fighters.*

Production

Model 83	NX7133 (A–8129)
Model 89	NX7134 (A–8128)
F4B–1	A–8130 to A–8156
F4B–2	A–8613 to A–8639
	A–8791 to A–8809
F4B–3	8891 to 8911
F4B–4	8912 to 8920
	9009 to 9053
	9226 to 9263
	9719
F4B–4A	2489 to 2511 (cvtd from P–12s)
P–12	29–353 to 29–361
XP–12A	29–362
P–12B	29–329 to 29–341
	29–433 to 29–450
	30–29 to 30–87
P–12C	31–147 to 31–242
P–12D	31–243 to 31–277
P–12E	31–553 to 31–586
	32–1 to 32–76
P–12F	32–77 to 32–101
Model 100	NS–21
	NX872H
	873H
	NX874H
Model 100A	247K
Model 100E	Two for Thailand
Model 100F	X–10696
Model 218	X–66W
Model 256	Fourteen for Brazil
Model 267	Nine for Brazil

Top: *The P–12J in Wright Field markings, where it was test-flown with an experimental bomb sight.*

Right: *Two of the nine Model 267s delivered in 1933 to the Brazilian Air Force.*

XP–7
(Model 93)

As INDICATED by the manufacturer's Model number, the XP–7 actually appeared after the Model 66/XP–8, although its US Army designation was allotted earlier. The sole XP–7 was produced by converting the 16th and last aircraft of the Army's PW–9D order, which was retained at the Boeing factory for experimental installation of a 600hp Curtiss V–1570 Conqueror engine. It was delivered to the Army Air Corps in September 1928. Although a heavier unit—it was basically a larger, higher-powered development of the D–12 engine fitted to production PW–9s—the Conqueror increased the top speed of the XP–7 by some 8mph over the standard PW–9, and plans were made to order four more P–7s for comprehensive Army trials. By that time, however, the Models 83 and 89 had made their appearance. Since they clearly offered a greater development potential, the XP–7 programme was cancelled and the prototype restored to PW–9D standard.

Specification

SPAN	32ft 0in
LENGTH	23ft 5in
HEIGHT	8ft 2in
WING AREA	260sq ft
GROSS WEIGHT	3,260lb
MAX SPEED	168mph
CRUISING SPEED	134mph
ENDURANCE	2hr

Production
28–41 (cvtd from PW–9D)

The XP–7 (Model 93) prototype, a Conqueror-engined conversion of a PW–9D airframe.   [USAF

Model 95

DESIGN OF the Boeing 95 represented, in effect, an updating of the Model 40 concept for a single-seat biplane produced specifically for the carriage of air mails and other express goods. Based on the operating experience of Boeing Air Transport and Pacific Air Transport, it differed chiefly from the earlier design in being a single-bay, staggered-wing biplane with angular horizontal tail surfaces, and in employing the steel-and-dural form of fuselage construction developed for the Model 83 and 89 fighters. All-metal ailerons were fitted to the upper wings, and the tail surfaces were also of metal; the remainder of the wings, and the rear fuselage, were fabric-covered. One express and three mail compartments, with a total capacity of 89cu ft, were incorporated in the fuselage and permitted the carriage of 1,610lb of cargo. The pilot's open (but heated) cockpit was situated aft of the mail area, and the aircraft was powered by a 525hp uncowled Hornet radial engine.

A total of 25 Boeing 95s was built, of which the first made its maiden flight on December 29, 1928. Boeing Air Transport took 20 of them, starting in January 1929, and one was sold to National Air Transport, also a part of the BAT organisation. The remaining four were purchased by Western Air Express. With one of its Model 95s—C–397E, converted into a two-seater as R–397E—Boeing acquired its first experience of in-flight refuelling. Bearing the legend 'Boeing Hornet Shuttle' on its fuselage, this aircraft made a number of long-distance flights across America by refuelling from a modified Boeing 40B–4 or Douglas C–1 tanker aircraft. Another, fitted with a Wasp engine, was known as Model 95A, but this version did not go into production. Several more Model 95s, after ending their airline service days, were sold to Honduras and other Latin American countries, where they were employed as light bombers.

Specification

SPAN	44ft 3in
LENGTH	31ft 11in
HEIGHT	12ft 1in
WING AREA	490sq ft
GROSS WEIGHT	5,840lb
MAX SPEED	142mph
CRUISING SPEED	120mph
RANGE	520 miles

Production

C–183E to C–192E
C–417E to C–426E
C–397E
C–412E to C–415E

XP–9
(Model 96)

US ARMY AIR CORPS interest in the evolution of a monoplane fighter was expressed in its Specification X–1623A issued on May 24, 1928, and five days later it signed a contract with Boeing for the design and construction of an experimental prototype to meet this requirement.

The aircraft, which was given the Boeing Model number 96 and the AAC designation XP–9, was a strut-braced, high-wing monoplane, powered by a 600hp Curtiss SV–1570 Conqueror engine and armed with two 0·50in machine-guns on the sides of the forward fuselage. Provision was also made for the carriage of two 122lb and five 25lb bombs. The fuselage was of all-metal semi-monocoque construction, the wings

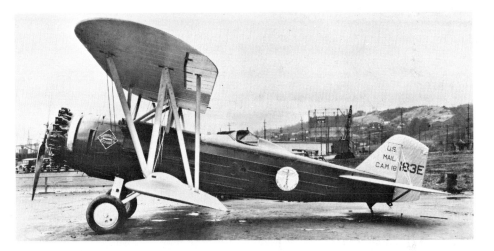

Top: *First Model 95 mailplane, photographed a few days before its first flight in December 1928.*

Right: *XP–9 after replacement of the original P–12 vertical tail by larger-area surfaces.*

being metal-framed with fabric covering.

Delivered by rail to the Army Test Center at Wright Field in September 1930, the XP-9 made its first flight there two months later, on November 18. Some initial control defects were improved somewhat by replacing the original P-12/F4B pattern fin and rudder with larger and more angular surfaces, but overall performance was below expectations and the pilot's view from his open cockpit aft of the wing trailing-edge was severely limited. As a result, the AAC option for five Y1P-9 service test aircraft was not taken up, and the project was abandoned.

Specification

SPAN	36ft 6in
LENGTH	25ft 1¾in
HEIGHT	9ft 10¼in
WING AREA	210sq ft
GROSS WEIGHT	3,623lb
MAX SPEED	213mph
CRUISING SPEED	180mph
RANGE	425 miles

Production
28-386

Monomail
(Models 200 and 221)

AFTER THE Model 102, Boeing continued its aeroplane numbering sequence with the Model 200, the intervening numbers having been allocated for company-designed aerofoil sections. Structurally and aerodynamically, the Model 200 represented a considerable advance over any previous Boeing design, for it was a smooth-skinned, all-metal cantilever low-wing monoplane, with a cowled engine and semi-retractable main landing gear. It was designed for the same mail- and cargo-carrying rôle as the Model 40 biplane, and functionally its layout showed little change in approach from that of its predecessor. The 220cu ft mail/cargo compartment was still located in the centre of the fuselage, with the pilot occupying a single open cockpit to the rear.

The Monomail, as the Model 200 was named, made its first flight on May 6, 1930. It utilised the same power plant—the 575hp Hornet B radial engine—as the Model 40B, and comparison of the two specifications indicates the extent by which performance was increased by virtue of the new streamlined design. The potential increase was much greater, had such niceties as variable-pitch propellers been available at the time to make the most efficient use of the engine. In this respect, however, the Monomail was ahead of its time, for with available propellers, whose pitch had to be pre-set on the ground before take-off, it could either take off

The colourful green, grey and orange Model 200 Monomail in May 1930.

The Model 221 Monomail, with six-passenger cabin in the forward fuselage.

with a full payload or cruise at high speed once airborne—but not both. By the time that variable-pitch propellers did become available, the Monomail was on the verge of replacement by later types of aircraft.

Because of these limitations the Model 200 did not go into production. However, on August 18, 1930, a second Monomail was flown. This had an 8in longer fuselage, in the front of which accommodation was provided for six passengers between the engine bay and the cargo hold. Apart from this modification, which earned it the new Boeing Model number 221, the second Monomail was identical with the first. Passenger conditions must have been somewhat claustrophobic, despite the ade-quate window area, for the external diameter of the cabin was only about 5ft. Nevertheless, the Model 221 was operated commercially for a time by Boeing Air Transport, and eventually both Monomails were modified for BAT service as Model 221As, by a further 2ft 3in extension of the front fuselage which increased the passenger capacity to eight in addition to the 750lb mail or cargo payload. The Model 200/221A, after conversion, was also used by Boeing for various test purposes and commercially by United Air Lines. One of the company tests concerned the development of an elevator trim-tab system, which not only improved the handling qualities of the Monomail but paved the way for the use of similar control systems on most other subsequent piston-engined Boeing designs.

Specification (Model 200)

SPAN	59ft 1½in
LENGTH	41ft 2½in
HEIGHT	16ft 0in
WING AREA	535sq ft
GROSS WEIGHT	8,000lb
MAX SPEED	158mph
CRUISING SPEED	135mph
RANGE	530 miles

Production
Model 200   NX725W
Model 221   NC–10225

XP–15 and XF5B–1
(Models 202 and 205)

QUITE EARLY in the production lifetime of the P–12/F4B series of fighters for the US Army and Navy, Boeing began, as a private venture, to prepare for the time when a departure would be required from the traditional biplane fighter format that had survived since World War I. At that time the company had already evolved two streamlined all-metal monoplane designs, the XP–9 fighter prototype and the commercial Model 200 Monomail. Feeling perhaps that a less radical approach might be more acceptable to the military, the company first projected the Model 97, which in essence was a parasol monoplane derivative of the P–12/F4B, arrived at by eliminating the lower wings. In the event, this design was not built; a subsequent decision favoured after all the adoption of all-metal construction, and a new design, the Model 202, was evolved whose fuselage was based on the constructional methods used in the XP–9.

Two months after its first flight in January 1930 the Boeing 202 was loaned to the USAAC, who gave it the Army designation XP–15. A near-identical machine (Boeing Model 205) had been delivered for evaluation in the previous month to the US Navy; this became known as the XF5B–1. Both aircraft initially had the small-area, angular vertical tail surfaces of the early P–12/F4B series, and were outwardly identical save for the deck

Model 205 (XF5B–1) naval prototype, virtually identical to the Model 202/XP–15, in its original form.

arrester hook on the heavier Navy prototype. The Boeing 205 was powered by an SR–1340C Wasp engine developing 480hp at sea level; the SR–1340D in the Model 202 gave 450hp at 8,000ft. Both prototypes were eventually given engine ring cowlings and the larger, rounded-shape fin and rudder designed for the Model 218.

As recorded under the P–12/F4B entry, later production models of those fighters made use of constructional techniques and materials employed in the Models 202 and 205. The latter types themselves, however, did not go into production, principally because they did not advance the performance from that of the biplane fighters in anything but outright speed.

Specification

SPAN		30ft 6in
LENGTH		21ft 0in
HEIGHT		9ft 4in
WING AREA		157sq ft
GROSS WEIGHT	(XP–15)	2,746lb
	(XF5B–1)	3,419lb
MAX SPEED	(XP–15)	190mph
	(XF5B–1)	171mph
CRUISING SPEED	(XP–15)	160mph
	(XF5B–1)	145mph
RANGE	(XP–15)	421 miles
	(XF5B–1)	690 miles

Production

XP–15	X–270V
XF5B–1	X–271V (A–8640 later)

Model 203

FIRST FLOWN on July 1, 1929, the Boeing 203 was a two/three-seat training biplane, five examples of which were built for service at the Boeing School of Aeronautics at Oakland, California. Three of the aircraft were fitted with 165hp Axelson radial engines, and a fourth with a 145hp engine of the same manufacture. Construction consisted of a welded steel-tube fuselage and wooden wings, all fabric-covered, with two seats side-by-side in the front cockpit and a second, single-seat cockpit to the rear. In the training rôle, dual controls were fitted for the pupil in the front cockpit.

The fifth aircraft (actually the second machine on the line) was completed with a 165hp Wright J–6–5 radial engine, making its first flight on August 29, 1929. Because of the different power plant this was designated Model 203A, and in due course the other four machines were re-engined to this standard. During later service they were also given larger fin and rudder surfaces, similar in shape to those of the Model 218 fighter prototype. Two additional 203As were built in 1935–36, by students at the Boeing School, bringing total production to seven. Four of these aircraft remained in service at Oakland until 1942, when they were acquired by United Air Lines. The other three, after a further power plant change in 1941 (to 220hp Lycoming R–680 radials) and installation of suitable equipment, were employed at the School as Model 203B advanced trainers until America's entry into World War II. A fourth 203A/203B conversion was carried out after the other three. Two 203Bs which survived the war were still in use some years afterwards, modified for crop-dusting duties.

Specification

SPAN	34ft 0in
LENGTH	24ft 4in
GROSS WEIGHT	2,625lb
MAX SPEED	108mph
CRUISING SPEED	92mph
RANGE	400 miles

Production

Model 203	NC976H to NC979H
Model 203A	NC587K
	NC12748
	NC13392

Third Model 203, prior to delivery to The Boeing School of Aeronautics, with Axelson engine and original vertical tail.

B–9
(Models 214, 215 and 246)

EVERY SO OFTEN in the course of military aircraft development there appears a bomber design which, by the performance increase which it exhibits in its own class, causes a substantial reappraisal of the prevailing state of the art in fighter design. One such aeroplane was the Boeing B–9, initiated as a private venture under the company Model numbers 214 and 215. Monomail influence was readily apparent in the aerodynamic cleanness and all-metal construction of the new bomber, and in its use of a semi-retractable main landing gear, although it still clung to a few such archaic concepts as open cockpits and an externally-carried bomb load. One particular innovation was the introduction of control surface servo-tabs—the first on an American warplane—necessitated by the high speeds and surface loadings inherent in the new design. Outwardly, the two prototypes were virtually identical, the major difference being between the 600hp Curtiss GIV–1510C Vee-type engines of the Model 214 and the 600hp P & W Hornet radials of the Model 215. The latter was the first of the two to fly (on April 13, 1931) and to be evaluated by the Army Air Corps, receiving the military designation XB–901 before purchase and YB–9 afterwards. The Model 214, following its first flight on November 5, 1931, was purchased as the Y1B–9, evaluated and then re-engined with a similar power plant to the 215/YB–9.

The Models 214/215 carried a crew of five men, two occupying nose and dorsal open positions and each manning a ring-mounted pair of 0·50in machine-guns. Immediately behind the nose gunner (who was also the bombardier) were two cockpits in tandem for the two pilots; the fifth crewman, the radio operator, was accommodated below and ahead of the pilots, inside the forward fuselage. Design warload consisted of two 1,100lb bombs.

When it bought the two prototypes, in August 1931, the US Army at the same time ordered for service trials five examples of a developed version with more efficient Hornet engines and a number of structural and equipment changes. The new engines were of the Y1GISR–1860B version, rated at 600hp at 6,000ft; defensive armament was reduced to two single 0·30in calibre guns, and the warload amended to four 600lb bombs; and the vertical tail surfaces were of a modified shape. With these changes, the developed version received the Boeing Model number 246 and the Army designation Y1B–9A. Delivery was made

between July 1932 and March 1933, following the first flight by a Y1B-9A on July 14, 1932.

Unfortunately for Boeing, its high hopes for substantial B-9 production orders were not realised. These went instead to the Martin B-10 and B-12, whose performance was even better than that of the B-9. Nevertheless, the very existence of such advanced bombers was enough to promote a corresponding surge in the development of fighter aircraft that could maintain the required degree of superiority over them. In this field, too, Boeing also had a large stake, with its Model 248 design which became the P-26 Army fighter.

Specification (Y1B-9A)

SPAN	76ft 0in
LENGTH	51ft 5in
WING AREA	960sq ft
GROSS WEIGHT	13,919lb
MAX SPEED	186mph
CRUISING SPEED	158mph
RANGE	1,150 miles

Production

YB-9	32-301 (initially NX-10633)
Y1B-9	32-302
Y1B-9A	32-303 to 32-307

Left: *The Conqueror-engined Model 214 bomber (Y1B-9).*

Top: *The Hornet-engined YB-9 prototype (Model 215) under test by the US Army.* [USAF

Right: *One of the five Y1B-9A (Model 246) service test aircraft, showing modified tail shape.*

XF6B–1/XBFB–1
(Model 236)

THE SINGLE-SEAT Model 236 was the last fixed-undercarriage biplane fighter to be designed by Boeing (although higher Model numbers were allotted to variants of earlier biplane designs), and in essence it represented the final attempt to update the excellent F4B–4. Design was started in 1931, and was centred on the use of a two-row radial engine, the 625hp Pratt & Whitney R–1535 Twin Wasp Junior, all-metal wing ribs and spars, and a fully-faired, oleo-type main landing gear. A little less than three months after the first flight on February 1, 1933, the aircraft was delivered to the Navy for test purposes, subsequent changes including the installation of a modified engine cowling and of three-blade and variable-pitch propellers.

In addition to its fixed armament of two 0·30in machine-guns, the XF6B–1 could also carry one 500lb and two 115lb bombs beneath the fuselage and lower wings, and in March 1934 this resulted in the new bomber/fighter Navy designation XBFB–1 being allotted.

Specification

SPAN	28ft 6in
LENGTH	22ft 1½in
HEIGHT	10ft 7in
WING AREA	252sq ft
GROSS WEIGHT	4,283lb
MAX SPEED	185mph
CRUISING SPEED	170mph
RANGE	525 miles

Production
A–8975

Model 247

WITH THE Model 247, Boeing at last capitalised on the new design and constructional trends which had been evident in the Monomail and the B–9. When the first Boeing 247 made its maiden flight on February 8, 1933, it marked the beginning of a new era in passenger air travel, at speeds more than 50mph faster than the standard types of airliner then in service. Moreover, a rarity at that time, this was a production aeroplane: there had been no separate prototype, and United Air Lines (formed from the Boeing Air Transport System) had in the previous year—while the project was still in the mock-up stage—placed a substantial order for no fewer than 60 of these sleek twin-engined transports to completely re-equip its fleet.

The Boeing 247 was of all-metal construction, the entire exterior having a light alloy skin. Another innovation was the provision of pneumatic rubber de-icing boots on the wing and tail leading-edges. Powered by two Wasp radial engines, each developing 550hp at 5,000ft, the 247 had accommodation for 10 passengers (at 40in seat pitch) and carried a crew of two pilots and a stewardess. Compartments in the nose and aft of the passenger cabin

Left: *Boeing's last biplane fighter design, the XF6B–1, photographed in January 1933.*

Top: *Boeing 247* City of Renton, *in UAL insignia.*

Right: *Boeing 247D, last production example, operated by United Air Lines.*

provided 125cu ft of space for passengers' baggage and up to 400lb of mail. Externally, the initial production Model 247 was distinguishable from later versions by its undercut cockpit windscreen and narrow-chord engine cowling rings. Sixty-one of this version were built, 59 of them as part of the UAL order and the other two for Deutsche Luft Hansa, the German airline.

One example (NC13300) was completed in 1933 as the Model 247A, a combined executive/research aircraft ordered by United Aircraft Corporation's Pratt & Whitney Division and powered by two of the Division's 625hp Twin Wasp Junior engines. Making its first flight on September 14, 1933, it was delivered early in the following November and continued to be used by P & W until after World War II.

There were no Models 247B or 247C built, the next (and only other major) variant being the Boeing 247D, of which 13 were built. This model had geared Wasp engines, in long-chord NACA cowlings and driving variable-pitch propellers, a backward-sloping cockpit windscreen, and fabric-covered tail control surfaces. These modifications were originally flight-tested on the very first 247 (re-designated 247E for the purpose) and were later carried out (except, on occasion, that to the windscreen) on all the original American-bought Model 247s, improving their performance considerably. One Model 247D, with additional fuel tanks installed in the cabin, was flown by Col Roscoe Turner and Clyde Pangborn to second position in the transport section and third in the overall speed section of the 1934 MacRobertson air race from London to Melbourne. Afterwards it was returned to

UAL, its original purchaser, and restored to standard for normal airline service. Another 247D was recovered from UAL by Boeing and converted in January 1937 as the personal, armed transport of a Chinese warlord. Designated Model 247Y in its new form, it had increased fuel capacity, a six-seat cabin, and an armament of three 0·50in machine-guns, two fixed in the nose and one on a ring mounting aft of the cockpit.

After the entry of the US into World War II a total of 27 Boeing 247Ds (including the entire surviving UAL fleet, except for one aircraft retained as a flying research laboratory) were impressed for military service. They were given the Army designation C-73 during this service, the survivors being released for civilian duty again in 1944. Eight others were used during the war by the Royal Canadian Air Force, of which one was later transferred to the RAF and became, in October 1944, the first aeroplane to make a fully-automatic landing, with ILS equipment linked to the Minneapolis Honeywell autopilot.

Specification

SPAN	(247)	74ft 0in
	(247D)	74ft 0in
LENGTH	(247)	51ft 4in
	(247D)	51ft 7in
HEIGHT	(247)	15ft 5in
	(247D)	12ft 1¾in
WING AREA	(247)	836sq ft
	(247D)	836sq ft
GROSS WEIGHT	(247)	12,650lb
	(247D)	13,650lb
MAX SPEED	(247)	182mph
	(247D)	200mph
CRUISING SPEED	(247)	155mph
	(247D)	189mph
RANGE	(247)	485 miles
	(247D)	745 miles

Production

247	NC-13301 to NC-13359
	D-AGAR
	D-AKIN
247A	NC-13300
247D	X-12272
	NC-13360 to NC-13370
	One for China

The final Model 247D, photographed in the mid-1960s while in use as a flying laboratory by the present United Air Lines.
[via S. P. Peltz

P-26 series
(Models 248, 266 and 281)

HAVING ESTABLISHED the all-metal monoplane design approach via the Monomail, the B-9 bomber and the Boeing 247 airliner, it was inevitable that the company should apply the same philosophy to the evolution of a new fighter. Whereas the other three types had been evolved entirely as private ventures, however, the fighter design was evolved with assistance from the Army Air Corps, and the P-26 which resulted (known affectionately as the 'pea-shooter') was one of the most distinctive monoplane fighters of the 1930s. The basic design, undertaken in 1931, was of Boeing origin; completion of three Model 248 prototypes was financed from company funds, with some design features, the engine, instruments and military equipment contributed by the USAAC. Two were flying prototypes, the second machine being used for static testing. While still Boeing property, the three machines were tested by the Army under the designation XP-936; after purchase they were redesignated successively, as their status changed, as XP-26, YIP-26 and finally P-26. The first flight was made on March 20, 1932.

Despite the modernity of the monoplane layout, the Model 248 still embodied a number of performance-inhibiting features, notably the extensive external wire bracing above and below the wings, a non-retractable (though well-streamlined) landing gear, and an open cockpit. Power plant was the 522 hp SR-1340E version of the well-tried Wasp engine, fitted with a narrow-chord NACA cowling ring, and provision was made for one or two machine-guns and a small under-fuselage bomb load. A retractable-gear variation, with fully-cantilevered wings, was developed as the Model 264/YP–29; this is described separately.

First production version of the Model 248 was the P–26A (Boeing Model 266), differing from the prototypes in having a revised internal wing structure and a minor alteration to the main landing gear fairings. In January 1933 the US Army ordered 111 P–26As; the first of these was flown on January 10, 1934, and deliveries were completed by the end of the following June. Service aircraft were fitted with radio and flotation gear, and, retrospectively, with deeper cockpit headrests. A more significant improvement, prompted by service experience, was the introduction of wing flaps, primarily to help reduce the P–26A's 73mph landing speed. The 600hp R–1340–27 version of the Wasp engine was installed in the P–26A, which served as the standard fighter of the 1st, 16th, 17th, 18th, 20th, 32nd and 37th Army Pursuit Groups in the US, Hawaii and the Panama Canal Zone.

The initial P–26A contract was augmented by an order for a further 25 fighters. Two of these were completed as P–26B/Model 266A, with SR–1340–33 fuel-injection engines and wing flaps, and delivered in June 1934 for service testing. The remaining 23 aircraft (P–26C/Boeing Model 266) initially had P–26A engines with minor modifications to the fuel system. Later, they were brought up to P–26B standard, though without any change in designation.

By the time of the attack on Pearl Harbor

One of the two XP–936 (Model 248) flying prototypes, later redesignated XP–26.

Boeing P–26As of the US Army Air Corps' 94th Pursuit Squadron. [Gordon S. Williams

the P–26 series, still based overseas, was no longer in first-line squadron service, having been replaced by Seversky P–35 and Curtiss P–36A fighters. Most of them were then sold, to Panama, the Philippines and Guatemala. Some Philippine Army Air Force P–26As were in action at the outset of the Pacific war, and the Guatemalan Air Force was still using the type (including some ex-Panamanian machines) 10 years after the war ended.

Prior to World War II Boeing also built 12 examples of an export version of the P–26A, known as the Model 281. The first of these was flown on August 2, 1934, flaps being fitted to all 12 aircraft before their export in 1935–36 to China (11) and Spain (1). The Chinese 281s were used in action against Japanese invaders in 1937.

Above: *P–26B, showing the wing flaps introduced on this version.* Below: *Ten of the 11 Model 281 fighters built for China in 1935–36.*

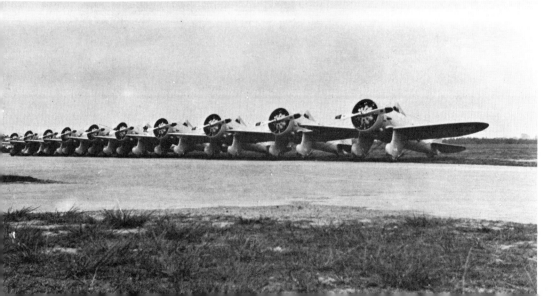

Specification (P–26C)

SPAN	27ft 11½in
LENGTH	23ft 9in
HEIGHT	10ft 0½in
WING AREA	150sq ft
GROSS WEIGHT	3,075lb
MAX SPEED	235mph
CRUISING SPEED	200mph
RANGE	635 miles

Production

XP–26	32–412 to 32–414
P–26A	33–28 to 33–138
P–26B	33–179 to 33–180
P–26C	33–181 to 33–203
Model 281	Eleven for China
	One for Spain

YP–29
(Model 264)

IN BETWEEN the design of the Model 248 and the production of the P–26A, Boeing prepared two other prototype fighter designs with such improved features as fully-cantilevered wings, a retractable main landing gear, and an enclosed cockpit. The second of these designs, although it bore an earlier Model number, was the Boeing 264. The other (described separately) was the Model 273. Three Boeing 264 prototypes were built, the first of them flying on January 20, 1934, with a 600hp R–1340–35 Wasp engine. During the next two months it was flight-tested at Wright Field, under the designation XP–940, before being returned for modification. At Army request, an open cockpit then replaced the long and narrow original enclosure, and a drag ring was substituted for the NACA-type engine cowling. In this form the aircraft was known as the YP–29A, the designation YP–29 having meanwhile been allotted to the second Model 264, which had been completed with a larger and more roomy 'glasshouse' cockpit canopy.

Like the P–26A, the Model 264 had an unfamiliarly high landing speed, and the Army asked for wing flaps to be added to the YP–29 prototype. After further company and Army testing the Y was dropped from the designation of this machine, and later the aircraft was assigned to the NACA for research work.

The Army still disliked even the roomier enclosure of the YP–29, and so the third prototype, the YP–29B, was built from the outset with an open cockpit. However, although the Model 264 was appreciably faster in level flight than the P–26 fighter, the added weight of its wheel retraction mechanism and internal wing bracing had an adverse effect upon other aspects of its performance and Army plans for placing a production contract were cancelled.

Specification (P–29)
SPAN	29ft 4½in
LENGTH	24ft 11¾in
WING AREA	176sq ft
GROSS WEIGHT	3,518lb
MAX SPEED	250mph
CRUISING SPEED	212mph
RANGE	800 miles

Production
YP–29	34–23
YP–29A	34–24
YP–29B	34–25

YP–29 (Model 264), with 'glasshouse' cockpit enclosure.   [Peter M. Bowers collection

XF7B–1
(Model 273)

ESSENTIALLY, the Boeing 273 was the Naval counterpart of the Model 264/P–29, though chronologically it preceded the Army fighter and was designed to a Navy specification, whereas the Model 264 was a private-venture design in which the Army collaborated. The Model 273—the first cantilever low-wing monoplane carrier fighter to be considered by the US Navy—won the competition from three other competitors, and a prototype was ordered in March 1933. When this aircraft, designated XF7B–1, made its first flight on September 14, 1933, it already embodied split trailing-edge wing flaps and a variable-pitch propeller for the 550hp SR–1340–30 Wasp engine—the first time these features had been incorporated in a Boeing design from the outset. Armament consisted of two 0·30in machine-guns. Originally, the prototype had an enclosed cockpit of the type fitted to the XP–940, but the Navy shared the Army's dislike of this feature and an open cockpit was substituted. For carrier operations, the landing speed was

considered to be too high, and so a third flap was added, beneath the wing centre-section. Even then, the XF7B–1 still landed at 70mph, and this, combined with inadequate manoeuvrability and other operational shortcomings—compared with contemporary Navy biplane fighters—led the Navy to decide against quantity production. During test-flying in March 1935, a sharp pull-out from a 415mph dive seriously weakened the structure of the aircraft, and in view of the Navy's rejection of the type the repair of the airframe was not felt to be worth while.

Specification

SPAN	31ft 11in
LENGTH	27ft 7in
HEIGHT	7ft 5in
WING AREA	213sq ft
GROSS WEIGHT	3,651lb
MAX SPEED	233mph
CRUISING SPEED	200mph
RANGE	750 miles

Production
9378

XB–15
(Model 294)

IN APRIL and May 1934 the US Army Air Corps issued two requirements which were to involve Boeing in the design of the two largest and heaviest aeroplanes thus far evolved in the history of the company. The first of these requirements was for an experimental long-range bomber, although the XBLR–1 designation applied at the time of the contract was amended to XB–15 during construction of the prototype when the 'Bomber, Long Range' category was dropped by the USAAC. Boeing's submission, the Model 294, was not only the largest and heaviest company product but the largest and heaviest aircraft ever built in the US up to that time.

The Model 294 design was drawn up, and mocked up, around the use of four 1,000hp Allison V–3420 Vee-type engines. These, however, were not available in time, and the XB–15 prototype made its first flight, on October 15, 1937, with a quartet of similarly-rated Pratt & Whitney R–1830–11 Twin Wasp two-row radials. Even with these its performance was below that anticipated for its military rôle, although good enough for it later to set world-class payload-to-height and distance-with-payload records.

Because of its great size and tremendous range, the XB–15 was able to introduce a number of new and/or interesting features. The 10-man crew needed to fly the aircraft and man the six machine-guns operated in

XF7B–1 prototype, with original cockpit enclosure and underwing fairings behind the retracted wheel positions.

watches, as on a ship, and so bunks and cooking facilities were installed to allow the off-duty members to rest and eat between duties. The wing roots were so thick that there was space for a tunnel behind the engine nacelles, from where the flight engineer could service the engines while in flight. Two petrol-driven generators provided electrical power for many of the accessory systems, and double wheels were fitted to the main landing gear units. Design bomb load, all carried internally, was 8,000lb.

Its relatively poor performance as a bomber—especially in comparison with the later B–17—led to the XB–15 being relegated to research flying, but after America's entry into World War II a new use was found for its tremendous load-carrying capability. Redesignated XC–105, it was converted as a cargo transport, in which capacity it survived almost to the end of the war.

Specification

SPAN	149ft 0in
LENGTH	87ft 7in
HEIGHT	18ft 1in
WING AREA	2,780sq ft
GROSS WEIGHT	37,709lb
MAX SPEED	200mph
CRUISING SPEED	152mph
RANGE	5,130 miles

Production
35–277

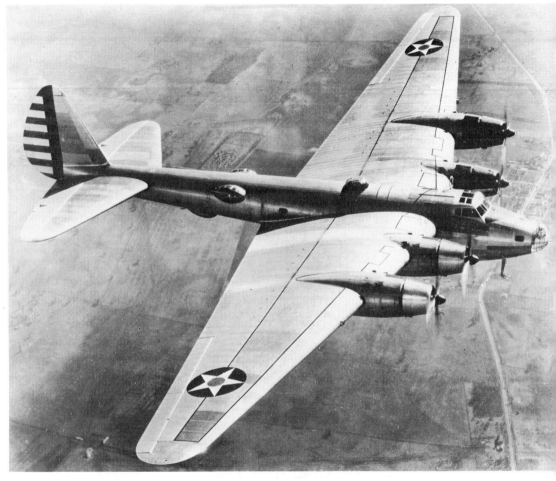

Largest American landplane of its time, the XB–15 was first flown in October 1937.

B-17 Flying Fortress
(Model 299)

INHABITANTS of Germany during the years 1942–45 might possibly require some convincing that the Boeing B–17 Flying Fortress was conceived originally as a defensive weapon; yet such indeed was the case. And that usually perspicacious British journal *The Aeroplane* must often have had cause, during those years, to reflect wryly upon its comment, made in the Autumn of 1940, that 'As fighting machines they are in fact obsolete in any country in the World'.

In May 1934, when the US Army Air Corps made known its requirements for a new, multi-engined anti-shipping bomber, the rôle of air power as an offensive weapon was still little appreciated and ill-defined. Moreover, the vesting of the offshore defence rôle with the Army was felt keenly by the US Navy, which later strongly opposed the adoption of the new aircraft. By August 1934, after some two months of intensive design work, Boeing was ready to begin building a prototype of its Model 299 bomber project. This was for a four-engined aircraft, whereas the term 'multi-engined' had hitherto been generally interpreted to mean 'twin-engined'. Having established that a four-engined design would not be considered ineligible, however, Boeing began in earnest to complete the Model 299 prototype in time for the Army competition date of August 1935. The design of this aircraft was particularly significant in that—unlike the XB–15, which was then under development—the object of the additional power was to enhance performance with the type of

warload normally carried by twin-engined bombers, rather than to carry a heavier load within the same modest performance envelope as earlier bombers.

The prototype Boeing 299 emerged as a clean, low-wing monoplane, powered by four 750hp Pratt & Whitney S1EG Hornet radial engines. Carrying an eight-man crew, it was armed with five defensive 0·30in machine-guns (one each in the nose, dorsal, ventral and two waist positions) and its eight 600lb bombs were stored completely internally. It made its first flight on July 28, 1935, and a little more than three weeks later was delivered to the Army for initial service trials. The delivery flight from Seattle to Wright Field, 2,100 miles away, was made non-stop at an average speed of more than 232mph—at that time an unprecedented performance for a large aircraft, and one which earned the 299 much excited attention from the national press. Unfortunately, the prototype was destroyed on October 30, 1935, when it crashed after taking off with the elevator controls inadvertently locked. Although thereby disqualified from the competition, it had already given sufficient indication of its potential worth, and in January 1936 Boeing was awarded an Army contract for a service trials batch of 13 YB–17s (Boeing Model 299B, later Y1B–17) and one airframe for static testing. These differed from the prototype in having 1,000hp Wright R–1820–39 Cyclone radial engines and a crew of six; the static test machine was in fact completed as a high-altitude flying prototype (Y1B–17A, Boeing 299F), its engines being of the R–1820–51 version fitted with turbo-superchargers. Twelve of the Y1B–17s

underwent service evaluation by the Army's 2nd Bombardment Group at Langley Field, with whom they remained (as plain B–17s) after the trials were completed. Six of them made a 5,260-mile flight from Miami to Buenos Aires in 1938, with only a single refuelling stop. This was typical of several long-distance flights across the USA and to Central and South America in 1938–39. In August 1939 the Y1B–17A, carrying an 11,000lb payload, set an altitude record of 34,000ft and a 621-mile closed-circuit speed record of 259·4mph.

Because of continued Army/Navy conflict over responsibility for coastal defence, and the generally modest appropriations at the time for Army equipment, it was not until 1938 that the first production order was placed, and even this was for the conservative quantity of 39 aircraft, designated B–17B (originally Boeing Model 299E, later changed to 299M). These had the R–1820–51 power plant, but incorporated various improvements, chief among which were a modified nose section and larger-area flaps and rudder. In 1939 a further contract was placed for 38 B–17Cs (Boeing Model 299H), in which the 1,200hp R–1820–65 version of the Cyclone was installed. In these aircraft, the two lateral gun blisters were omitted and the ventral blister was replaced by a larger 'bathtub' fairing. Other improvements included the provision of self-sealing fuel tanks and armour protection for the crew.

In March 1940 an agreement was made to release 20 of the B–17Cs to the RAF (which named them Fortress Mk I) in return for operational information obtained from their use in the European Theatre of

Operations. (Both Boeing and the US Army called the B–17 Flying Fortress, a name registered by the company as a trade mark before the prototype's first flight. The RAF, apparently considering the first half of this description self-evident, simply called it the Fortress.) The B–17Cs were followed by 42 B–17Ds (also Model 299H), which carried an additional crew member and incorporated a revised electrical system and engine cowl flaps. In addition, most of the B–17Cs remaining in US service were brought up to the same standard and re-designated B–17D. The RAF Mk Is, having sustained fairly heavy losses, were diverted to Coastal Command or Middle East squadrons. The USAAF also sustained early losses, including 18 B–17C/D in the first Japanese air attacks against the Philippines; by mid-March 1942, 26 Australian-based aircraft were the only B–17s in the Western Pacific. The 20 Fortress Is (given the Boeing Model number 299U) were delivered in 1941, and the assessment of information based on their initial use for high-altitude day-light missions over Germany prompted the development by Boeing of the Model 299–O, of which the initial production version was the B–17E.

The B–17E, the first example of which was flown on September 5, 1941, marked an extensive redesign of the bomber in the

Top: *An historic prototype—the Boeing 299, forerunner of the B–17 Flying Fortress.*

Centre: *A B–17C Fortress I, painted by Boeing in RAF markings before delivery. The inaccurate serial AM528 was later corrected to AN528.*

Left: *A 1941 study of a USAAC B–17D.*
[Peter M. Bowers

light of current operational knowledge. It represented a determined effort to increase the battleworthiness of the B–17 by increasing the armour and armament. A power-operated front upper turret was installed, a similar turret (or, in the final 400 aircraft, a ball turret) in the ventral position and, for the first time, a turret in the tail. The total number of guns was thus increased to nine, all except one of which were of 0·50in calibre. Overall length, compared with the B–17C, was increased by 5ft 11in, and keel area was substantially increased, to improve high-altitude control and stability for bombing, by the introduction of a huge curving dorsal extension of the tail fin, a feature which characterised all subsequent models in the B–17 series. Boeing production of the B–17E totalled 512, of which 45 were supplied under Lend/Lease to the RAF as the Fortress Mk IIA. The B–17E also equipped the 97th Bombardment Group of the US Eighth Air Force, which in August 1942 made the first raids on European targets by UK-based units of the USAAF. Other B–17Es saw extensive service in the Pacific theatre of war. Variants of the B–17E included one converted to a passenger transport (designation XC–108) and used as a staff aircraft by General Douglas MacArthur; another, the XC–108A, was converted as a freighter; and one (XB–38) was flown experimentally in May 1943

Top: *B–17E in a left bank, displaying the enlarged dorsal fin area introduced by this model.*

Right: *Vega-built Boeing B–17F.*   [USAF

66

with 1,425hp Allison V–1710–89 liquid-cooled Vee-type engines, a project abandoned after the loss of the prototype in a crash a month later.

The vast production resources of the American aviation industry, once the US became actively involved in World War II, are strikingly illustrated by the rise in output of the B–17 series. Production of the first four models, B–17B to E, totalled 631 aircraft; from 1942, when manufacture of the B–17F began, 12,085 examples of this model and the B–17G were built, including contributions from the Douglas and Vega factories, to make the Fortress America's second most important bomber type in terms of the numbers built. By June 1944, at the peak of this production, Boeing's Seattle plant alone was turning out 16 B–17Gs every 24 hours.

Altogether, 3,405 examples were built of the B–17F version. Although embodying numerous internal improvements, this was outwardly similar to the B–17E except for R–1820–97 engines, paddle-blade propellers, and a moulded Plexiglas nose which increased the overall length by 11in. Provision was made for underwing bomb racks, increasing the possible long-range warload to 8,000lb, and there were variations in the nose armament of some aircraft. Boeing-Seattle built 2,300 B–17Fs, the others being completed by Douglas at Long Beach (605) and Vega Aircraft

Top: The 'chin' turret of the B–17G.

Right: Allison-powered Fortress test-bed, designated XB–38.

Corporation at Burbank (500) in new factories built specifically for B–17 production. 'One-off' B–17F conversions included the YC–108 VIP transport and the XC–108B experimental fuel-ferrying aircraft. Nineteen B–17Fs were supplied to the RAF (as Fortress Mk IIs), and a further 41 were converted for photographic reconnaissance duties with the designations F–9, F–9A and F–9B. The F–9C (10 delivered) was a similar conversion of the B–17G, the final production version.

To improve the bomber's ability to repel attacking enemy fighters, the B–17G was equipped with a two-gun power-operated 'chin' turret under the nose; this feature was also added later to a number of B–17Fs in service and to the final 86 B–17Fs on the Douglas production line. The B–17G became the major production model, of which no fewer than 8,680 examples were completed—4,035 by Boeing, 2,395 by Douglas and 2,250 by Lockheed-Vega. The RAF received 85 B–17Gs, which it designated Fortress III and allocated to Coastal Command. During and after the war, 47 others (and one B–17F) were acquired by the US Navy, by now officially responsible for shore-based maritime patrol. Suitably disarmed and modified, 31 of these went into USN

Top: *B–17 test-bed with nose-mounted Wright T35 turboprop engine.* [Howard Levy

Centre: *B–17G/PB–1W in post-war service with the Peruvian operator Andoriente.* [Air-Britain

Left: *PB–1G Flying Fortress of the US Coast Guard.* [Air-Britain

service as PB–1W early-warning aircraft; 17 others, equipped to carry a lifeboat beneath the fuselage, served with the US Coast Guard as PB–1Gs for air/sea rescue and iceberg reconnaissance. The former could be distinguished by the large APS–20 radome, usually beneath the centre of the fuselage but occasionally mounted above. The latter version followed the successful operation by the USAAF of a similarly equipped model, the B–17H. About 130 of these were scheduled to be produced by converting existing B–17Gs; only 50 such conversions are believed to have been made, though some B–17Gs in Europe were also adapted to carry lifeboats. Other B–17G conversions included two (Boeing Model 299–Z) which, while retaining their existing power plant, each had a turboprop engine installed in a modified nose. These tested, respectively, the 5,500hp Wright XT35 turboprop and the Pratt & Whitney XT34, the former aircraft being designated first EB–17G and later JB–17G. Other engines tested in B–17s included the Wright J65 turbojet (in a pod under the fuselage) and the Allison T38 and T56 turboprops in nose installations.

In an attempt to provide a heavily-armed escort for the wartime B–17 bomber formations, a number of B–17Fs were converted to B–40s, carrying a total of 14 machine-guns. One XB–40 prototype (on which the chin turret of the B–17G was developed) and 20 YB–40 conversions were made, together with four TB–40s for training. Unfortunately, they were too heavy to keep up with standard bomber B–17s once the latter had released their load, and this particular venture was therefore not pursued.

About 25 other B–17s, mostly Fs, were converted in 1944 to serve as BQ–7 radio-controlled flying bombs for use against U-boat pens and other deeply-fortified targets. It was in a BQ–7 that Joseph P. Kennedy Junior was killed, when the aircraft blew up during an operation from England before the crew could bale out.

After the war, a number of converted B–17F and B–17G aircraft, among them the Boeing 299AB executive transport conversion for TWA, operated non-commercial passenger-carrying services under a Limited Type Certificate. Seven others, from among 68 interned after force-landing in Sweden, were converted for use on Swedish scheduled airline services; and at least one was similarly converted for service with DDL, the Danish airline. More recently, in 1970 a B–17E was converted by Aero Flight Inc of Cody, Wyoming, as a borate bomber for use against forest fire outbreaks. Intended to prolong the airframe life of the aircraft after spares for the Cyclone engines are no longer available, this machine retains the rear portion of each Cyclone nacelle; into these are faired four 1,990ehp Rolls-Royce Dart 525 turboprop engines.

The grand total of B–17 production, which at Boeing ended in April 1945, was 12,731. Of these, Boeing built 6,981, Douglas 3,000 and Vega 2,750.

Other experimental or redesignated models not listed above included the following:

CB–17 Unarmed VIP transport, converted from various B–17 series.
DB–17P Drone director aircraft, converted from B–17G.

FB–17 Photographic version (later RB–17; *not* a redesignation of F–9 series).
QB–17M and N Radio-controlled (usually target) drones.
RB–17 'Restricted' (WWII) category, assigned in October 1942 to B–17B/C/D models withdrawn from bomber duties.
RB–17G Reconnaissance category (introduced 1948), aircraft formerly designated F–9C or in FB–17 series.
SB–17 Search and rescue version (B–17H redesignated).
TB–17 Trainer.
VB–17 Staff transport (similar to CB–17).

Specification

SPAN	(B–17C)	103ft 9in
	(B–17E)	103ft 9in
	(B–17G)	103ft 9in
LENGTH	(B–17C)	67ft 11in
	(B–17E)	73ft 10in
	(B–17G)	74ft 4in
HEIGHT	(B–17C)	15ft 5in
	(B–17E)	19ft 2in
	(B–17G)	19ft 1in
WING AREA	(B–17C)	1,420sq ft
	(B–17E)	1,420sq ft
	(B–17G)	1,420sq ft
GROSS WEIGHT	(B–17C)	46,650lb
	(B–17E)	53,000lb
	(B–17G)	65,500lb
MAX SPEED	(B–17C)	323mph
	(B–17E)	317mph
	(B–17G)	287mph
CRUISING SPEED	(B–17C)	250mph
	(B–17E)	210mph
	(B–17G)	182mph
RANGE	(B–17C)	2,400 miles
	(B–17E)	2,000 miles
	(B–17G)	2,000 miles

Blackburn Shark

SEVEN Shark II torpedo-spotter-reconnaissance biplanes, built in Britain by the Blackburn Aircraft Co Ltd, were delivered in 1936 for service with the Royal Canadian Air Force. Following receipt of these aircraft, the RCAF decided to acquire an additional 17 Sharks, and manufacture of these (except for the stainless steel wing spars, supplied from England) was undertaken in 1938–39 by the new Boeing-Canada factory, erected in 1937 at Sea Island Airport, Vancouver, British Columbia. These 17 aircraft were designated Shark III; they had a glazed canopy over the two/three-man crew, similar to that fitted to the British Mk III, and were operable from either wheeled or twin-float landing gear. Main differences from the British Shark III included substitution of an 800hp Bristol Pegasus IX radial engine in place of the 700hp Armstrong Siddeley Tiger VI, and omission of the deck arrester hook.

Specification
SPAN	46ft 0in
LENGTH	35ft 2¼in
HEIGHT	12ft 1in
WING AREA	489sq ft
GROSS WEIGHT	7,870lb
MAX SPEED	152mph
CRUISING SPEED	118mph
RANGE	550 miles

Production (Boeing production only)
514 to 524
545 to 550

Boeing (Canada)-built Shark III torpedo seaplane.
[Peter M. Bowers collection

Stratoliner
(Model 307)

THE STRATOLINER, America's first four-engined pressurised airliner, originated with the projected Boeing Model 300, which was undertaken in parallel with the Model 299 as a transport counterpart to the new bomber. The Boeing 300 was not built, but was developed into the Model 307, which made use of the wings, power installation and tail surfaces of the B–17C Flying Fortress. The only modification to any of these components was the addition of leading-edge slots to the outer wing panels. Power plant was the GR–1820–G102A version of the Wright Cyclone, giving 1,100hp for take-off and 900hp at 17,300ft. The fuselage, however, was entirely new, being fully pressurised and of a circular cross-section that added 3ft 6in to the overall span compared with the B–17C. Accommodation within this capacious structure was for a crew of five (including a flight engineer) and 33 passengers, the cabin being convertible into a 16-berth sleeper transport with space also for nine other passengers in reclining sleeper chairs.

Although designed to a December 1935 requirement, the Stratoliner was not put into production until 1937, following the receipt of orders from Pan American Airways for three aircraft and from Trans-continental and Western Air (TWA, now Trans World Airlines) for five. A pro-

Top: *Prototype Model 307 Stratoliner, with original vertical tail surfaces.*

Right: *TWA Stratoliner, showing underwing flap hinge fairings.*

duction line of ten aircraft was then started in the newly-opened Plant 2. The first of the PanAm aircraft, which served as the prototype, flew for the first time on December 31, 1938, but was lost in March 1939 while being test-flown by a KLM pilot. Construction of the remainder continued, flight testing being completed by later machines. The only major modification found necessary was to increase the vertical tail area. For a time the second PanAm aircraft (c/n 1995) flew with a straight dorsal fairing to the original fin, but eventually an entirely new tail form was adopted, consisting of a redesigned rudder and a continuous-curve fin fairing which resulted in an outline much resembling that introduced later on the B–17E Flying Fortress. Delivery of the first three aircraft, to Pan American, was made in 1940.

For the first time, prefix letters were introduced by Boeing to differentiate between variants of the same aircraft built for different customers. Thus the Pan American Stratoliners were designated S–307 (though equally often referred to as PAA–307), while the TWA machines were SA–307B. The latter possessed a number of detail differences, the principal ones being the installation of GR–1820–G105A engines and the presence of triangular flap hinge fairings beneath the wings.

A ninth aircraft (actually the fourth off the production line) was completed for millionaire Howard Hughes as the SB–307B and delivered in July 1939. Originally, Hughes planned to use this for a round-the-world record attempt, but when that plan was cancelled following the outbreak of war in Europe the eight additional fuel tanks were removed from the cabin, which

The 'Flying Penthouse' Stratoliner built for multi-millionaire Howard Hughes.

was fitted with an ultra-luxurious interior for Hughes's use as a personal transport. At this stage the production-style fin and rudder were substituted for the smaller fin first fitted, and the original engines were replaced by 1,600hp R–2600 Twin Cyclones. Neither Hughes nor its next owner, Texas millionaire Glenn McCarthy, made much use of it, and when sold to another purchaser late in 1963 it had flown only 500 hours in 24 years.

By contrast, a considerable amount of use had been made of the eight airline 307s. The Pan American trio, flown by PAA crews, operated on military transport schedules (though without military designations) between the USA and South America from shortly after America's entry into World War II. They were returned to PAA in late 1944, and were still achieving

an average 8½ hours flying a day in 1946, when they carried some 70,000 passengers on services between Miami, Havana, Nassau and Barranquilla. One was later purchased for the President of the Republic of Haiti, and was still being operated on his behalf by the Haitian Air Corps in the early 1960s. The other two were subsequently operated in Ecuador by Aerovias Ecuatorianas, but all eventually returned to the USA.

The five TWA Stratoliners were also 'drafted', early in 1942. They operated under the military designation C–75 with the Army's Air Transport Command, and were named Apache, Cherokee, Comanche, Navajo and Zuni during their Army service. They, too, were flown by airline crews, and before their demobilisation in the Autumn of 1944 had amassed nearly 45,000 hours of wartime flying, during which they crossed the Atlantic some 3,000 times. Prior to their wartime service they had already flown some 4,500,000 miles without accident. Before returning to commercial operation, they were refurbished by Boeing to an extent that earned them the revised Model number SA–307B–1. They re-emerged with 1,200hp GR–1820–G666 engines, B–17G wings (with leading-edge slots added), nacelles and tail surfaces, and a B–29-type electrical system. Operating with the cabin pressurisation equipment removed, they were able to seat up to 38 passengers, and in 1946 were achieving an average daily utilisation of $10\frac{3}{4}$ hours, flying five round trips a day between New York and Kansas City. In April 1951 all five were sold to the French airline Aigle Azur, with whom they continued to serve for a number of years. One subsequently operated with Airnautic of France, and another with Air Laos, and the other three operated a service on behalf of the Armistice Commission between North and South Vietnam.

Above: *Stratoliner C–75* Zuni *in Army warpaint.* [USAF

Below: *A surviving Stratoliner photographed in the 1960s with a French operator.* [S. P. Peltz

Specification

SPAN	107ft 3in
LENGTH	74ft 4in
HEIGHT	20ft 9in
WING AREA	1,486sq ft
GROSS WEIGHT	42,000lb
MAX SPEED	246mph
CRUISING SPEED	220mph
RANGE	2,390 miles

Production

S–307	NC–19901 to NC–19903
	NC–19910
SA–307B	NC–19905 to NC–19909
SB–307B	NC–19904

Model 314

DESIGN OF the Boeing 314 commercial flying-boat actually began before that of the Model 307 Stratoliner, following discussions held with Pan American Airways in 1935, but a Model number was not allocated until the Spring of 1936, when the design was submitted to the airline for approval. As the Stratoliner had been evolved to make use of B–17 components, so the Model 314 design was based on the use of the wings and the horizontal tail surfaces of the larger XB–15 bomber. Power plant consisted of four 1,500hp Wright GR–2600 Double Cyclone engines, installed in XB–15-type nacelles. Fuel capacity was 4,200 US gallons. Accommodation within the flying-boat hull provided for a crew of up to 10 persons, with a minimum capacity for 74 daytime passengers or 40 in the sleeper configuration. For on-the-water stability, sponsons were preferred to wingtip floats; they had the added advantages of providing fuel storage space and serving as loading/boarding platforms.

In July 1936, Pan American placed an order for six Boeing 314s, and the first of these—there was no separate prototype—made its initial flight on June 7, 1938. Originally, this machine was built with a single fin and rudder. When greater directional control was found to be needed, this was first achieved by substituting a pair of outrigged oval fins and rudders; to these, later still, was added a central fin of similar shape and area to the original combined surfaces, and this configuration became standard on subsequent production aircraft. Delivery of all six

to PAA was made between January and June 1939. Their first operations were on the North Atlantic route: an air mail service was inaugurated on May 20, 1939, followed by a regular passenger service—the first ever across the Atlantic—just over a month later, on June 28. Subsequently they also flew trans-Pacific services from San Francisco to Hong Kong. PanAm's use of 'Clipper' fleet names for its aircraft led to them becoming known in a general sense as 'Boeing Clippers', but this was never an official company name for the 314.

Pan American's original order was followed by a contract for a further six aircraft, incorporating modifications designed to improve their range and performance. Known as Model 314As, these had 1,600hp Double Cyclone engines with larger-diameter propellers, an extra 1,200 US gallons of fuel, and a modified interior layout seating three additional passengers.

The first example was flown on March 20, 1941. In 1942, five of the original six 314s were brought up to the same standard and redesignated 314A. Meanwhile, however, following the outbreak of war in Europe, three aircraft from the second PAA order (c/n 2081, 2082 and 2084) were purchased before delivery by BOAC for wartime trans-Atlantic service. These were given military camouflage, but operated with British civil registrations and airline fleet names as G–AGBZ *Bristol*, G–AGCA *Berwick* and G–AGCB *Bangor* respectively. In May 1941 they joined other BOAC flying-boats on the Foynes–Lagos sector of the so-called 'Horseshoe route' to the Antipodes, though the majority of their subsequent wartime flying was done on Atlantic routes. *Berwick* brought Winston Churchill back to England from Bermuda in January 1942 following his official visit to the United States and Canada—to be met by half a

dozen Hurricanes sent to intercept the un-announced 'hostile'! The three Boeings served with BOAC throughout the war, eventually being sold to Transocean Airlines via the General Phoenix Corporation in April 1948.

Of the American-operated 314s, *Anzac Clipper* had a narrow escape on December 7, 1941: en route for Singapore, it was only an hour's flight from Hawaii when the captain received news of the attack on Pearl Harbor. At this time *Pacific Clipper* was in Auckland, New Zealand, and because of the new situation in the Pacific completed its return in a westbound direction via the Netherlands East Indies, Ceylon, Karachi, Khartoum and New York to San Francisco. In 1942, PAA's remaining three 314As and one of the 314/314As were requisitioned for Air Transport Command of the USAAF, by whom they were designated C–98. One 314A was returned to PanAm in November 1942; about a year later the other three aircraft were transferred to the US Navy, which also acquired two others direct from the airline. These five flying-boats, known to the Navy simply as B–314s, retained their civil registrations and were flown by airline crews. In January 1943 *Dixie Clipper*, accompanied by *Atlantic Clipper*, flew President Roosevelt to Casablanca for his famous conference with

Left: *The first Model 314 flying-boat under construction at Seattle.*

Top: *First Model 314 with ultimate tail configuration.*

Right: Boeing 314 Bristol, *one of three acquired by BOAC early in World War II.*

Winston Churchill; *American Clipper* provided the escort on the homeward journey.

Only one of the Boeing flying-boats was lost during the war, though not to enemy action. This was *Yankee Clipper*, destroyed in a landing accident at Lisbon in February 1943. In November 1945 *Honolulu Clipper* force-landed in the Pacific as a result of engine failure. Although undamaged, it was struck a few days later by the ship sent out to secure it, and had to be written off. Such was the seaworthiness of the huge 'boat that it took 1,300 rounds of 20mm ammunition to send it to the bottom.

PanAm's 314 operations ceased in April 1946. The surviving aircraft—apart from *Atlantic* and *Pacific*, cannibalised to provide spares—were acquired by the charter operators Universal Airlines and American-International Airways. One was sunk by gunfire in the Atlantic in October 1947, following a forced landing and similar consequences to those that ended *Honolulu*'s career. Six of the remaining machines were beached in 1949 and scrapped in 1950; the seventh was destroyed in harbour by a storm in 1951.

Specification (Model 314)

SPAN	152ft 0in
LENGTH	106ft 0in
HEIGHT	27ft 7in
WING AREA	2,867sq ft
GROSS WEIGHT	82,500lb
MAX SPEED	193mph
CRUISING SPEED	183mph
RANGE	3,500 miles

Production

Model 314	NC–18601 to NC–18606
Model 314A	NC–18607 to NC–18612

Kaydet series (PT–13, –17, –18, –27 and N2S)
(Stearman Model 75)

WHEN THE Stearman Aircraft Company became a Boeing subsidiary in 1934, it placed in production that year its Model 73, a derivative of the Stearman Model C series of biplanes of 1926–30 and based on the Model 70 prototype which had been completed in December 1933. From this beginning was to grow a family of primary training aircraft of which, by 1945, no fewer than 8,584 examples had been built for the US services and other customers, plus spares equivalent to a further 1,762 of these aircraft. Sixty-one Model 73s, with 225hp Wright R–790–8 Whirlwind 9 (J–5) radial engines, were delivered in 1935–36 to the US Navy under the designation NS–1; 17 others, and 78 Model 76s, were built for export between 1935 and 1941. The Model 76 was, in essence, a slightly larger version of the Model 75. Variants produced, mainly for advanced training or light military duties, included the 76D1 for the Argentine Navy, 76C3 for the Brazilian Air Force, and 76B4 for the Venezuelan Air Corps. A variety of radial engines was fitted in these aircraft, including the R–760 Whirlwind 7 (J–6), 420hp R–975–E3 Whirlwind 9 (J–6), Lycoming R–680, and 320hp Pratt & Whitney R–985–T1B Wasp Junior.

Line-up of Stearman NS–1 primary trainers at Corry Field, Pensacola. [US Navy

The major member of the family was the Model 75, whose civil-registered prototype appeared in 1936 and was awarded its Approved Type Certificate on June 24 of that year. Evaluation by the US Army resulted in an order for 26, with 215hp Lycoming R–680–5 engines, as PT–13 primary trainers. Follow-on orders were placed for 92 PT–13As (220hp R–680–7 engines) and 155 PT–13Bs (280hp R–680–11 engines); six of the latter were converted subsequently to PT–13Cs for night and instrument flying training. In 1939, during the course of this production, the Stearman Company became the Wichita Division of Boeing.

The largest individual production model of the entire series—3,769 were built—was the Model A75N1, basically similar to the PT–13A except for the installation of 220hp Continental R–670–4 or –5 engines. Principal Army version of this was the PT–17, from which were converted 136 PT–17As (night and instrument training), three PT–17Bs (for pest control) and one PT–17C. The Navy received 250 as N2S–1s and 455 as N2S–4s, the intervening designations being applied to 125 N2S–2s (Lycoming R–680–8 engines, Boeing/Stearman Model number B–75) and 1,875 N2S–3s (Model B–75N1, identical to the A75N1/N2S–1 except for later-series R–670–4 engines).

The US Army's original PT–17 order had meanwhile been followed by others for a further 150 aircraft, bearing the manufacturer's Model number A75J1 to signify installation of a 225hp Jacobs R–755–7 engine. Six of these were equipped as PT–18As for night and instrument instruction, the remainder being completed as PT–18 daytime trainers. Three hundred Model D–75N1s, basically similar to the PT–17 except for the addition of 'winterisation' equipment, were built under Lend/Lease arrangements for the Royal Canadian Air Force, by whom they were named Kaydet, a name that came to be applied, unofficially, to all aircraft of this type during World War II. Because of the equipment changes and the terms of their

Stearman 76 D1 in the insignia of the Argentine Naval Aviation Service.

purchase, the Canadian machines were given the USAAF designation PT–27 for recording purposes. One PT–27 was flown experimentally with an enclosure over its tandem cockpits, but this feature did not gain general acceptance.

Last variant of the Model 75 series to be built for the US services was the Model E–75, powered by the Lycoming R–680–17 engine and evolved for both the Army and Navy to use without the necessity for interchanging equipment. Development of this version was through the PT–17C conversion mentioned above. Production, curtailed at VJ-day, amounted to 895 for the Army as the PT–13D and 873 for the Navy as the N2S–5.

Versions of the Model 75 produced for export or commercial customers included the A75B4 (five for Venezuela, delivered in November 1941, with 320hp Wright R–760–E2 engines); the A75L3, with 225hp Lycoming R–680–B4D, of which 43 were built in 1940–41 for Brazil (20), the Philippines (12), Venezuela (7) and Parks Air College (4); the A75L5 (two ex-Navy N2S–4s, rebuilt 1946 for the Republic of China with 190hp Lycoming O–435–11 horizontally-opposed engines); and 20 A75N1/N2S–3s and B75N1/PT–17s, also for China, with Continental R–670–4 radial engines.

After World War II, thousands of Model 75s became available for civilian purchase, and were widely employed as private or display aircraft or for agricultural duties with a variety of individual modifications by their respective owners. Particularly popular was the replacement of their existing engines by another war-surplus item, the Pratt & Whitney Wasp Junior

Left: *Stearman PT–13 primary trainer of the US Army Air Corps.*

Above: *Line-up of Stearman PT–17s awaiting delivery to the USAAC.*

Right: *PT–13 floatplane in post-war service with the Philippine Air Force.*

engine, which offered about twice the power of the original installations. More than 4,000 Model 75s were recorded on the US civil register for 1950; half this number were still current nine years later, and several hundreds were still flying in North America in 1970. As recently as 1968, the design of the Model 75 was taken as the basis for a 'new' agricultural aircraft, the MA–1, engineered by Air New Zealand on behalf of Murrayair of Hawaii—a remarkable tribute to a still-useful aeroplane whose first appearance was made 35 years earlier.

Stearman Model 75, much-modified, used in Canada as a glider tug.   [J. Hutchinson

Specification (PT–13)

SPAN	32ft 2in
LENGTH	24ft 0¼in
HEIGHT	9ft 2in
WING AREA	297sq ft
GROSS WEIGHT	2,810lb
MAX SPEED	122mph
CRUISING SPEED	107mph
RANGE	440 miles

Production

Model 75	X75L3
PT–13	36–2 to 36–27
PT–13A	37–71 to 37–114
	37–232 to 37–259
	38–451 to 38–470
PT–13B	40–1562 to 40–1741
	41–787 to 41–861
PT–13D	42–16846 to 42–16995
	42–17057 to 42–17063
	42–17080 to 42–17095
	42–17097 to 42–17101
	42–17115 to 42–17134
	42–17150 to 42–17182
	42–17184 to 42–17190
	42–17200 to 42–17219
	42–17227 to 42–17863

PT–17	40–1742 to 40–1891
	41–862 to 41–1086
	41–7867 to 41–9010
	41–25202 to 41–25736
	41–25741 to 41–25747
	41–25749 to 41–25801
	42–15896 to 42–16723
N2S–1	3145 to 3394
N2S–2	3520 to 3644
N2S–3	3395 to 3519
	4252 to 4351
	05235 to 05434
	07005 to 08004
	37988 to 38437
N2S–4	27960 to 28058
	29923 to 30146
	34097 to 34101
	34107 to 34111
	37856 to 37967
	37978 to 37987
	55650 to 55771 (not built)

N2S–5	38438 to 38610
	43138 to 43637
	52550 to 52626
	61037 to 61097
	61105 to 61120
	61137
	61143 to 61155
	61176 to 61190
	61224
	61232 to 61240
	61261 to 61267
PT–18, –18A	40–1892 to 40–2041
PT–27	FD968 to FD999
	FJ741 to FJ999
	FK100 to FK108
A75B4	Five for Venezuela
A75L3	Twenty for Brazil
	Seven for Venezuela
	Twelve for Philippines
	Four US civil

Douglas DB–7

To MEET delivery requirements for large numbers of this twin-engined attack bomber, Boeing-Seattle was engaged to undertake production of the DB–7 under licence from the Douglas Aircraft Company. Its contribution to the DB–7 programme began with a May 1940 contract to complete 240 aircraft originally ordered by the French government. Outstanding French orders for aircraft were taken over by Britain after the fall of France, and the DB–7Bs received the RAF designation Boston III. The first Boeing-built DB–7B was flown on July 24, 1941, and delivery of all 240 aircraft was made between October 30 that year and the end of March 1942. Some of them are believed to have been among those diverted to the Soviet Air Force after its entry into the war on the Allied side. Others were later repossessed by the USAAF for conversion to A–20C Havocs, used in the USA as trainers for the Douglas P–70 two-seat night fighter.

This process was continued when the USAAF awarded Boeing a contract for an additional 140 aircraft built from the outset as Havocs. These also were designated A–20C, and, since they were intended originally for delivery to the RAF under Lend/Lease, were fitted with British equipment. In fact, however, the majority were diverted to, and used by, the USAAF itself.

Specification (A–20C)

SPAN	61ft 4in
LENGTH	47ft 4in
HEIGHT	17ft 7in
WING AREA	464sq ft
GROSS WEIGHT	19,750lb
MAX SPEED	342mph
CRUISING SPEED	280mph
RANGE	1,050 miles

Production (Boeing production only)

Boston III	AL263 to AL336
	AL337 to AL502
A–20C	41–19589 to 41–19728

Boeing-built Douglas DB–7B (Boston III) in RAF markings.

Waco CG–4A

THE MOST extensively-built troop- and cargo-carrying glider employed by any of the combatants in World War II was the Waco CG–4A, of which a total of 13,909 were built by 16 US manufacturers between 1941–43. Of this total, the comparatively modest quantity of 750 was ordered from the Cessna Aircraft Company of Wichita. Cessna in turn sub-contracted the entire batch to Boeing, who built them in the new Plant 2 at Wichita during 1942, in between tooling-up for initial production of the B–29 Superfortress. After the war, hundreds of surplus CG–4As were sold, complete in their packing cases—and so cheaply that customers frequently bought them *for* the cases and threw the gliders away!

Specification

SPAN	83ft 8in
LENGTH	48ft 4in
HEIGHT	12ft 7in
WING AREA	852sq ft
GROSS WEIGHT	7,500lb
MAX TOWING SPEED	120mph

Production (Boeing production only)
42–61101 to 42–61460
42–61821 to 42–62210

Top: *Waco CG-4A troop glider built at Boeing-Wichita during World War II.*

Right: *Boeing (Canada)-built PB2B-2 flying-boat.*

Consolidated PBY and PB2B series

ONE OF THE TWO major Allied flying-boats in service during World War II, the Consolidated PBY Catalina (an RAF name, later adopted also by the US Navy) was the subject of extensive wartime production. In addition to those built by the parent company, manufacture was also undertaken by the Naval Aircraft Factory at Philadelphia and by two Canadian concerns, Boeing Aircraft of Canada Ltd, of Vancouver, and Canadian Vickers Ltd of Montreal.

Boeing-Canada's contribution amounted to a total of 362 of these flying-boats, beginning in 1942 with a batch of 55 amphibians for the Royal Canadian Air Force. Equivalent to the US Navy's PBY–5A model, these were named Canso by the RCAF, to whom they were delivered between October 1942 and July 1943. Delivery then continued, without a break, of 240 aircraft equivalent to the PBY–5. Of these, 200 were for the RAF, 75 as a direct purchase and 125 as Lend/Lease equipment bearing the USN designation PB2B–1. To the RAF they were known as Catalina IVB; seven of them were delivered to the Royal Australian Air Force. Thirty-

four of the other PB2B-1s were assigned to the RNZAF, the remainder being retained by the US Navy. Deliveries of this second batch of flying-boats were completed in October 1944.

Meanwhile, the Naval Aircraft Factory had developed its PBN-1 version of the PBY-5, identifiable by its much taller fin and rudder, and Boeing-Canada completed its Catalina production by building 67 aircraft of a similar type as PB2B-2s, delivering them between September 1944 and March 1945. Fifty-nine were for the RAF (Catalina VI), although all but 13 were actually delivered to the RAAF. The remaining eight were used both by the US Navy and (still with their USN designation) by the USAAF.

XBT-17 (Stearman X-91) with Wasp Junior engine.

Specification (Catalina IVB)

SPAN	104ft 0in
LENGTH	65ft 1in
HEIGHT	18ft 6in
WING AREA	1,400sq ft
GROSS WEIGHT	33,133lb
MAX SPEED	187mph
CRUISING SPEED	115mph
RANGE	2,690 miles

Production (Boeing production only)

Canso A	9751 to 9805 (RCAF)
Catalina IVB	JX270 to JX437
	JX586 to JX617
	NZ4023 to NZ4056
	44205 (USN)
	44220 to 44223 (USN)
Catalina VI	JX618 to JX662
	JX828 to JX841
	44238 to 44245 (USN)

XBT–17
(Stearman Models X–90 and X–91)

THIS TWO-SEAT monoplane, Stearman's first after a decade and a half of biplane construction, was a dual-purpose design, intended to offer one basic airframe with a choice of alternative power plants for, respectively, the primary training (X–90) and basic training (X–91) rôles. For the former, it was to have a 225hp Lycoming R–680–B4D radial engine, and for the latter a 450hp Pratt & Whitney R–985–AN–1 Wasp Junior. Only one prototype was completed, in 1941, this being fitted in turn with each engine selected. In its Wasp-powered form it was purchased by the USAAF, as the XBT–17, for evaluation; but by this time the shortage of aluminium supplies, which the aircraft's mixed wood-and-metal construction had been intended to circumvent, had been overcome, and the Army decided against adding an extra training type to its existing inventory for this feature alone.

Specification

SPAN	35ft 9½in
LENGTH	27ft 9½in
HEIGHT	8ft 5in
WING AREA	201sq ft
GROSS WEIGHT	4,150lb
MAX SPEED	190mph
CRUISING SPEED	160mph

Production

X–90	X–21924
X–91	42–8726 (XBT–17; cvtd from X–90)

XA–21
(Stearman Model X–100)

THE X-100 was a Stearman design, evolved as a contender in a US Army competition for a twin-engined, three/four-seat light attack bomber. It carried a later company designation and constructor's number than the X-90/X-91, but in fact the single example built was completed and flown early in 1939, some two years before the trainer and shortly before Stearman Aircraft Company became the Wichita Division of Boeing. In March of that year it was flown to the USAAC's Wright Field at Dayton, Ohio, where it was subsequently evaluated under the designation XA-21.

An all-metal shoulder-wing monoplane, the XA-21 was powered by two under-slung 1,150hp Pratt & Whitney R-2180-7 Twin Hornet radial engines—themselves still in the experimental stage—and had a tailwheel-type landing gear with electrically-retractable main units. Other notable features included a flush-riveted skin, fully-feathering constant-speed propellers, integral fuel tanks (capacity 450 US gallons), and sealed compartments in the fuselage, tail and outer wings to provide a safety margin of buoyancy in the event of a forced landing on water. Provision was made for an armament of six 0·30in machine-guns and an internally-stowed bomb load of 2,700lb. For maximum crew visibility, the entire upper portion of the fuselage nose was made up of glazed panels with an unbroken upper contour, but later this was modified to have a conventional 'stepped' cabin windscreen.

No production of either the XA-21 or the Twin Hornet engine was undertaken, the Stearman aeroplane thus being the only aircraft to have flown with this power plant.

Specification

SPAN	65ft 0in
LENGTH	53ft 0in
HEIGHT	14ft 0in
WING AREA	607sq ft
GROSS WEIGHT	18,230lb
MAX SPEED	257mph
CRUISING SPEED	190mph
RANGE	1,200 miles

Production
40–191

Left: *XA–21 (Stearman X–100), original nose configuration.*

Below: *Nose contours of the XA–21 after modification.*

XAT–15 Crewmaker
(Stearman Model X–120)

THE Stearman X–120 was designed to compete in a 1942 USAAF competition for a bombing crew trainer, and was, in effect, a 'mini-bomber' in itself. Like the XBT–17, it had been designed to avoid the use of strategic materials in its construction, especially aluminium alloys and castings; hence the welded steel-tube fuselage and the tail control surfaces were covered largely with fabric, while the wings and fixed tail surfaces were of wood with plywood covering. Carrying a crew of four, the XAT–15 was powered by two 550hp Pratt & Whitney R–1340–AN–1 Wasp radial engines, and had provision for internal stowage of ten 100lb bombs and a single 0·30in machine-gun. The gun could be installed in the power-operated dorsal turret or various other positions, and the entire concept of the design was to give pre-combat training to a bomber crew—pilot, navigator, bombardier and wireless operator/gunner—*as* a crew, after each member had undergone the individual training appropriate to his rôle. The first XAT–15 was delivered for tests in April 1942.

As events turned out, it was the Crewmaker's composite construction that brought the cancellation of Army contracts for 1,045 of these aircraft (including 325 by Bellanca and 360 by McDonnell). By the time production was due to have started the aluminium shortage had been overcome, the AT–15 appropriation was transferred instead to Fairchild's all-wooden AT–21 design, and the two XAT–15 prototypes remained the only examples to be completed.

Specification

SPAN	59ft 8in
LENGTH	42ft 4in
HEIGHT	13ft 1in
WING AREA	457sq ft
GROSS WEIGHT	14,355lb
MAX SPEED	207mph
CRUISING SPEED	185mph
RANGE	850 miles

Production
41–23162 to 41–23163

Boeing (Stearman) XAT–15 Crewmaker, first of two prototypes built.

XPBB–1 Sea Ranger
(Model 344)

THE Sea Ranger was another promising Boeing aircraft whose prospects of production were negated by changing wartime requirements. Much of the flying-boat experience gained with the Model 314 went into its design, and although different in planform the high aspect ratio wings of the Sea Ranger were very similar in aerofoil section and construction to those of the Boeing B–29 Superfortress.

The most remarkable aspect of the XPBB–1 prototype, which flew for the first time on July 9, 1942, was its outstanding size for a twin-engined aeroplane. The capacious fuselage housed a crew of 10, for whom living accommodation was provided for use during long patrols, and had space for a maximum bomb load of twenty 1,000lb bombs over short ranges. The Sea Ranger, was, however, primarily designed for long-range patrol, as evidenced by its name, its fuel capacity of 9,575 US gallons and its theoretical endurance of 72 hours. Accomplishment of such a performance, in an aircraft with a gross weight of more than 100,000lb, was made possible by the choice of two 18-cylinder Wright R–3350–8 Duplex Cyclone radial engines, each developing 2,000hp and driving a three-blade 'paddle' type propeller. Provision was also made for the use of JATO (Jet-Assisted Take-Off) gear. Power-operated ball turrets in the nose and tail each mounted a pair of 0·50in machine-guns.

Built in Plant 1, the prototype was assembled in a new Navy-built factory at Renton, on Lake Washington. It was taken to Sand Point in mid-January 1943

The XPBB–1 Sea Ranger, for the production of which the Renton factory was originally built.

for Navy tests, and plans were made for an initial production batch of 57 PBB–1s to be started at Renton, to where the prototype was returned on February 23, 1943. By then, however, the US Navy had decided that its operational requirements could be met by flying-boat types already in production. The PBB–1 contract was therefore cancelled, and the XPBB–1—inevitably, then, dubbed 'The Lone Ranger'—remained the only example of a potentially significant design.

Specification

SPAN	139ft 8½in
LENGTH	94ft 9in
HEIGHT	35ft 0in
WING AREA	1,826sq ft
GROSS WEIGHT	101,129lb
MAX SPEED	219mph
CRUISING SPEED	158mph
RANGE	4,245 miles

Production
3144

B–29 and B–50 Superfortress
(Model 345)

B-29

THE ORIGINS of the aeroplane that was to become the instrument to end World War II are traceable back to March 1938, three years and nine months before the nation that produced it became an active participant in the war. At that time, Boeing produced for the US Army Air Corps a design study—Model 334—for a pressurised development of the B–17 Flying Fortress with a tricycle landing gear. There was then no specific military requirement for such an aircraft, and the US Army was already having enough difficulty in securing appropriations for the B–17 itself. Nevertheless, it encouraged Boeing to keep the concept alive and up to date, and by July 1939 the company had arrived at the Model 334A—having in the meantime discarded an alternative project, the Model 333, for an aircraft with its four engines buried in a thick-section wing. In December 1939 a mock-up of the 334A was built, but a month later it became necessary to revise the specification in the light of combat experience during the early months of the war in Europe. The outcome of this revision was the Model 345, and by late August 1940 funds had been secured to cover the building of two prototypes (designated XB–29) and a third airframe for static tests. A third flying prototype was ordered in the following December.

The first XB–29 was flown on September 21, 1942, but already, by January of that year, the USAAF had placed orders for 14 YB–29 service test aircraft and 500 production B–29s; and a month later had announced an unprecedented industry-wide manufacturing programme for the new bomber involving Bell, North American and the Fisher Body Division of General Motors. By the time the first prototype flew, there were 1,664 B–29s on order. In the event, co-production of the B–29 was undertaken by Bell and Martin, with Fisher making sub-assemblies only; and the Navy-built Plant 2 at Renton, set up originally to manufacture the now-cancelled PBB–1 flying-boat, was used for exclusive production of the B–29A.

Although conventional in construction—all-metal, apart from the fabric-covered control surfaces—the B–29 nevertheless posed a production and modification problem on a scale unequalled by any other American aircraft during World War II. Peter M. Bowers, himself a Boeing engineer and author of the definitive *Boeing Aircraft since 1916* (Putnam & Co), refers to 'the truly heroic development programme that in four years designed, built, tested and perfected one of the most complex pieces of movable machinery ever made up to the time and trained the crews that put it in action over ranges never before attained in combat operations'; and this is no exaggeration. To start with, the B–29 was the first military aeroplane in the world to have pressurised compartments for all members of the crew, including the tail gunner. The guns themselves—ten 0·50in machine-guns and one 20mm cannon—were installed in five remotely-controlled turrets, sighted from positions within the pressurised areas; and division of the bomb load between two separate bays necessitated a control gear to release weapons alternately from the front and rear bays, to avoid upsetting the aircraft's CG balance.

The biggest single headache, however, resulted from the tremendous all-up weight of the aircraft. In 1942 it was the heaviest aeroplane in the world to go into production, and its narrow-chord wings, with their 11·5 aspect ratio, produced wing loading figures that caused the Army considerable anxiety. For a typical wartime gross weight of 124,000lb, the corresponding wing loading of the B–29 was 71·88lb/sq ft; by comparison, the B–17E then in production had a wing loading of only 37·32lb/sq ft even at its maximum overload weight of 53,000lb. However, the use of large-area Fowler flaps, adding 20 per cent to the total wing area when extended, minimised risk during take-off and landing; and by extensive wind tunnel research, and flight testing of small-scale replicas of the B–29 wings and tail on a Fairchild PT–19A 'guinea-pig' aircraft, Boeing were able to convince the Army that the bomber could perform its function safely as well as efficiently. Power plant of the bomber was the new Wright R–3350 Duplex Cyclone radial engine, fitted with twin turbo-superchargers and developing 2,200hp. The R–3350–13 model was installed in the XB–29, changing to –21 in the YB–29 and –23 in the B–29 production version. One YB–29, used by General Motors for engine tests, was redesignated XB–39 after being refitted with 2,100hp Allison V–3420 liquid-cooled engines.

The first public announcement of the Superfortress in action came following an attack on June 5, 1944, on railway marshal-

ling yards at Bangkok. This was made by aircraft based in India, to where they had been flown via the Atlantic and North Africa in the vain hope of concealing their presence in the Far East from the Japanese. In fact, the Japanese were already aware of their new opponent anyway, and less than a fortnight later, on the night of June 14/15, Superfortresses bombed targets in Japan itself, from advance bases on the Chinese mainland. From then on a mounting offensive was built up, reaching its peak after US forces recaptured the Marianas Islands, from where, eventually, 20 bomber groups were able to operate, sending formations of up to 500 B–29s in day and night raids against Japan. The most effective weapon was the incendiary bomb, against which the flimsy Japanese buildings were virtually defenceless: in the worst B–29 fire raid, against Tokyo, some 84,000 people died. The object of the offensive, following the pattern of that in Europe, was to soften up the enemy and reduce his resources prior to invasion of his homeland —and it is worth noting that, until April 1945, the B–29s generally operated without benefit of fighter escort. As events were to prove, however, invasion was unnecessary. Science had evolved the atomic bomb, and the Superfortress *Enola Gay* was chosen as the vehicle to deliver the first of these awesome weapons on the city of Hiroshima,

Top: *Unarmed XB–29 prototype taking off for its first flight.*

Centre: *B–29–BW Superfortress, most examples of which were delivered in natural metal finish.*

Right: *B–29B* Challenger, *built by Bell, was used by General 'Jimmy' Doolittle while in command of the US 8th Air Force on Okinawa.*

on August 6, 1945. The cryptically-named 'Little Boy' bomb totally destroyed 4·7 square miles of the city and killed more than 70,000 people. Three days later a second B–29, named *Bockscar*, dropped a second atomic bomb ('Fat Boy') on Nagasaki, and on August 15, 1945 (VJ-day) the Emperor of Japan surrendered to the Allies.

During their operations from China, three returning B–29 Superfortresses, after suffering damage, diverted to the Soviet Union, whose government—not then officially at war with Japan—interned them. From these aircraft the design bureau headed by Andrei Tupolev produced a 'Chinese copy' of the B–29, which became known as the Tu–4 bomber (NATO code name 'Bull'). The Tu–4 became standard bomber equipment with the Soviet Air Force for a time, and about 100 were supplied by the USSR to equip a strategic bombing force of the Chinese Air Force formed in 1951. In the Soviet Union, the Tu–4 was also the basis for a lengthy series of developments which included the Tu–70 troop transport ('Cart') and enlarged bomber designs with turboprop engines which led in the end to the swept-wing Tu–95 'Bear' bomber.

The ending of the war in the Pacific inevitably brought wholesale cancellations of all kinds of military equipment on order,

Top: *Wichita-built B–29, used in 1946–47 as launch aircraft for the Bell X–1 supersonic research aircraft.* [Bell Aerospace Company

Right: *Tu–70 Soviet transport aircraft, developed by the Tupolev design bureau from the B–29 Superfortress.*

and included among these were 5,092 B–29s. The final total actually built, including test aircraft, was 3,960: 2,756 by Boeing at Seattle (three XB–29s), Renton (1,119, all B–29As) and Wichita (1,634), 668 by Bell Aircraft Corporation at Marietta, Georgia, and 536 by The Glenn L. Martin Company at Omaha, Nebraska. At its production peak, Boeing-Wichita was manufacturing 85 of these aircraft a month.

Towards the end of the war, the lack of Japanese fighter opposition prompted the lightening of the B–29 by deleting all except the tail armament; 311 aircraft (all Bell-built, and re-designated B–29B) incorporated this modification. During 1945, 118 B–29s and B–29As, retaining their standard armament and bombing capability, were fitted with reconnaissance cameras and redesignated F–13 and F–13A. In the new designation system introduced in 1948 these became known as RB–29 and RB–29A respectively.

All subsequent B–29 variants, which carried suffix letters through to T (except I and O, for obvious reasons, and N, Q and R), were conversions or modifications

Top: *Three-point refuelling of RAF Gloster Meteor fighters by a KB–29M tanker.*
[Charles E. Brown

Centre: *Washington B. Mk 1 (B–29) bombers of No. 115 Squadron RAF during the early 1950s.*
[Ministry of Defence (RAF)

Left: *Equipped with A–3 airborne lifeboats and search radar, some Superfortresses were employed as SB–29 search and rescue aircraft by the US Air Force.*
[USAF

of existing airframes, and are summarised below:

EB–29B One B–29B (44–8411, named *Monstro*) modified for air-launching of McDonnell XF–85 parasite fighter. Five 'captive' flights made prior to first launch of XF–85 on August 23, 1948.

B–29C Assigned to B–29 intended for R–3350 engine development tests, but not taken up.

B–29D Improved and redesigned version, built as B–50A (*see below*).

XB–29E Fire control system test aircraft. One only.

B–29F Cold-weather trials with 'winterisation' equipment. Six conversions, later restored to original standard.

XB–29G Flying testbed for various General Electric turbojet engines. Normal power plant retained, the test engine being extended into the airstream, while the aircraft was airborne, on a flexible mounting installed in the bomb bay. One only.

XB–29H Armament test aircraft. One only, converted from B–29A.

YB–29J Originally test aircraft for R–3350–CA–2 fuel-injection engines. Two later became YKB–29J hose-refuelling tankers, and some became RB–29J photographic reconnaissance aircraft. Approximately six conversions.

B–29K Designation allotted originally for hose-refuelling tanker conversions, but applied instead to single B–29 used as cargo transport.

B–29L Designation allotted originally for hose-refuelling receiver conversions, but not taken up; conversions were instead designated B–29MR.

KB–29M Hose-refuelling tankers: 92 converted.

B–29MR Hose-refuelling receivers: 74 converted.

KB–29P Boom-refuelling tankers: 116 converted.

YKB–29T Triple-hose tanker, capable of refuelling three fighters at once. One only, converted from KB–29M.

The flight refuelling rôle was an important post-war one for the Superfortress, initially for its value in extending the range of the bomber itself and then as a support aircraft for the fighters of the USAF's Tactical Air Command and bombers of Strategic Air Command. Three pairs of KB–29M tankers, placed at appropriate points along the route, refuelled the B–50A *Lucky Lady II* when it made the first-ever non-stop round-the-world flight in 1949. Other post-war episodes in the B–29's career included the transfer of four to the US Navy in 1947, which were employed as P2B–1S long-range over-water search aircraft, and the loan of 88 others to the RAF (which named them Washington) from 1950–55 pending delivery of Avro Lincolns. One of the P2B–1Ss was modified later for use as 'mother-plane' for the Douglas D–558–II Skyrocket research aircraft. In addition to the XB–29G noted above, other B–29s were used to test-fly Pratt & Whitney engines, including the J42 and J48 turbojets, and an NACA ramjet.

Often neglected in accounts of the B–29's career is its contribution to the Korean war of 1950–53; yet B–29s were in action on all but 26 days of this three-year conflict, during which time they dropped 167,100 tons of bombs in 21,000 sorties, shot down 33 enemy fighters including 16 MiG–15s, with a further 28 MiGs damaged or probably destroyed. Total B–29 losses during the war were 34, of which only 20 were attributable to enemy action.

Specification

SPAN	141ft 3in
LENGTH	99ft 0in
HEIGHT	27ft 9in
WING AREA	1,739sq ft
GROSS WEIGHT	124,000lb
MAX SPEED	358mph
CRUISING SPEED	230mph
RANGE	3,250 miles

Production

XB–29	41–2 to 41–3
	41–18335
YB–29	41–36954 to 41–36967
B–29–BW	42–6205 to 42–6454*
	42–24420 to 42–24919
	44–69655 to 44–70154
	44–87584 to 44–87783
	45–21693 to 45–21872
B–29–MO	42–65202 to 42–65313
	42–65315 to 42–65401
	44–27259 to 44–27358
	44–86242 to 44–86473
B–29–BA	42–63352 to 42–63751
	44–83890 to 44–84152
B–29A	42–93824 to 42–94123
	44–61510 to 44–62328

* Includes five each completed by Bell and Martin.

B-50

Despite the heavy cancellations of B–29 orders at the end of World War II, plans already made for an improved version were enabled to continue. The improved model was originally to have materialised as the B–29D, built of a stronger and lighter aluminium alloy and powered by the 3,500hp Pratt & Whitney R–4360 Wasp Major, a 28-cylinder four-row radial engine. A B–29A was allocated to the engine manufacturer for flight testing of the new power plant, being redesignated XB–44 with the new installation. The 200 B–29Ds ordered in July 1945 had been cut to 60 after VJ-day; redesignation of these to B–50A was a piece of military sleight-of-hand performed to facilitate the approval of funds for a 'new' aircraft which might have been denied to a fresh model of a bomber so recently the subject of wholesale cancellations. The Boeing Model number 345–2 was given to the B–50 version.

The B–50A, apart from the innovations already mentioned, featured several improvements in equipment and systems, but the most noticeable outward change was the increase of some 5ft in the height of the vertical tail surfaces. First flight of a B–50A was made on June 25, 1947, and altogether 371 B–50s were built—80 B–50As, 45 B–50Bs, 222 B–50Ds (Boeing Model number 345–9–6) and 24 TB–50Hs (Model 345–31–26). The new company designation for the D version signified design changes that included a new one-piece moulded-plastic nose cone and provision for underwing auxiliary fuel tanks. For the TB–50H, an unarmed bombing and navigation trainer, it indic-

Above: *Second of the 59 production B–50A Superfortresses, recognisable instantly from the B–29 series by the taller tail surfaces.*

Below: *B–50D, with boom-type refuelling receptacle, underwing auxiliary tanks and one-piece nose transparency.*

ated deletion of the in-flight refuelling equipment, as well as the installation of training gear and three additional crew positions. The last TB–50H was delivered in March 1953.

Modifications and conversions of existing aircraft produced also the following variants:

TB–50A Bomber-trainer for B–36 crews. Eleven converted from B–50A, of which most later became KB–50J three-hose refuelling tankers.

EB–50B Manufacturer's tests (various). One only, converted from B–50B.

RB–50B Photographic reconnaissance: 44 converted from B–50B.

DB–50D One aircraft used for initial drop tests of Bell GAM–63 Rascal missile.

TB–50D As TB–50A: 11 converted.

WB–50D, WB–50H Weather reconnaissance. Converted from TB–50D and TB–50H (before they became KB–50s): number of conversions not known.

RB–50E Specialised photo-reconnaissance model: 14 modified from RB–50B.

RB–50F Special-duty model with Shoran (SHOrt RAnge Navigation) radar: 14 modified from RB–50B.

RB–50G Similar to RB–50F but with additional radar and B–50D nose: 15 modified from RB–50B.

KB–50J Triple-hose refuelling tanker for Tactical Air Command: 112 converted from B–50A or RB–50B, with two 5,200lb st General Electric J47 underwing turbojets in addition to normal power plant.

KB–50K As KB–50J, but converted (24 examples) from TB–50H.

Above: *KB–50 (converted B–50D) refuelling three F–100 Super Sabre fighters by the probe-and-drogue system.* [Flight Refuelling Ltd

Below: *B–50A used (in similar fashion to that of the XB–29G) as a jet engine test-bed.*

Other B–50s were used to flight test examples of the Pratt & Whitney J57 and Wright J65 turbojet engines.

As indicated by the addition of auxiliary jet power to the KB–50 variants during 1957–59, the Superfortress basic design, then 20 years old, was by that time outpaced both literally and tactically by the post-war generations of jet aircraft in service. The tanker variants began to be withdrawn from service in 1964, although a few were still operational in Vietnam a year or two after that date.

Specification

SPAN	(B–50D)	141ft 3in
	(KB–50J)	141ft 3in
LENGTH	(B–50D)	99ft 0in
	(KB–50J)	105ft 1in
HEIGHT	(B–50D)	32ft 8in
	(KB–50J)	33ft 7in
WING AREA	(B–50D)	1,720sq ft
	(KB–50J)	1,720sq ft
GROSS WEIGHT	(B–50D)	173,000lb
	(KB–50J)	179,500lb
MAX SPEED	(B–50D)	380mph
	(KB–50J)	444mph
CRUISING SPEED	(B–50D)	277mph
	(KB–50J)	367mph
RANGE	(B–50D)	4,900 miles
	(KB–50J)	2,300 miles

Production

B–50A	46–2 to 46–60
	47–98 to 47–117
B–50B	47–118 to 47–162
B–50D	47–163 to 47–170
	48–46 to 48–127
	49–260 to 49–391
TB–50H	51–447 to 51–470

94

C–97 Stratofreighter and KC–97

(Model 367)

ALTHOUGH it did not enter USAF service until 1948, the Boeing Stratofreighter was actually designed six years earlier, shortly after America's entry into World War II. Essentially, it bore the same relation to the B–29 that the Stratoliner had borne to the B–17, utilising the wings, power plant, landing gear and tail assembly of the bomber in association with an entirely new fuselage. In the case of the Stratofreighter, this took the form of a pressurised structure, with a 'double-bubble' cross-section, the upper (and larger) circle intersecting a lower one of the same diameter as the B–29. The cargo floor was located where the two portions intersected. In the upswept underside of the rear fuselage were clamshell loading doors, through which cargo could be loaded or driven up built-in ramps to the 74-foot-long upper hold. This could accommodate two light tanks, three fully-loaded 1½-ton trucks, 134 fully-equipped troops or 83 stretchers and four medical attendants. Separate doors provided access to the lower hold, and a crew of five was carried.

Three XC–97 prototypes were ordered in January 1942, but, because of the US aircraft industry's preoccupation with combat aircraft and with production of existing transport designs for its own and

Third aircraft of the initial production batch of C–97A Stratofreighters.

other Allied air forces, the completion of these proceeded at comparatively low priority. The first XC–97 (Boeing Model 367–1–1), powered by four 2,325hp Wright R–3350–57A engines, was flown on November 15, 1944. On January 9, 1945, carrying a 20,000lb payload, it made a non-stop flight of 3,323 miles from Seattle to Washington DC, in 6hr 4min at an average speed of 383mph. Six months later, the US Army ordered six YC–97s, three YC–97As and one YC–97B for service trials. The first YC–97 flew on March 11, 1947. This version differed from the XC–97 in having increased fuel capacity, modified engine nacelles and an improved electrical system, and was operated by Air Transport Command of the USAF on services to Hawaii. The YC–97As incorporated the same improvements that had been introduced on the B–29D/B–50A—Wasp Major engines, enlarged vertical tail, de-icing gear, 75ST aluminium alloy structure, etc—and the first of them flew a considerable number of hours during the Berlin Airlift of 1948. The sole YC–97B was essentially similar to the YC–97As, except that the clamshell loading doors were omitted, circular fuselage windows were added, and the interior was furnished as an 80-passenger luxury transport, complete with lounge and dressing rooms.

An initial production order for 27 C–97As was later increased to 50, the final 23 aircraft having an additional cargo door in the upper front fuselage. All C–97As carried search radar in a 'chin' radome, and had additional fuel tankage in the outer wings. Three were converted to KC–97As, to evaluate the aircraft as a flight refuelling tanker, which was to

A B–50D receiving fuel from one of the three KC–97As used to evaluate the latter type as a 'flying boom' tanker. [Flight Refuelling Ltd

become the aircraft's primary rôle. An improved form of Boeing Flying Boom (first developed on the KB–29P) was fitted, operated from a blister fairing added in place of the clamshell doors where the forward end of the boom joined the fuselage. After use for these tests they were restored to C–97A standard. Fourteen C–97Cs were built in 1951 for aeromedical evacuation duty in Korea, with reinforced cargo floors and minor internal improvements. These changes were retained in the KC–97E tanker, of which 60 were built with R–4360–35C (instead of –35A) engines and a total fuel load of 14,990 US gallons —nearly double that of the C–97A. Provision was made for the KC–97E to operate as a cargo transport if required, by removal of the 7,200-gallon upper-floor fuel tanks and Flying Boom gear and re-instatement of the cargo door. Production of the C–97 series ended in July 1956 after completion of 159 KC–97F and 592 KC–97G tankers, bringing to 888 the total of

C–97 series aircraft built. Both of these models were powered by 3,500hp R–4360–59B engines, but the latter had 700 US gallon underwing auxiliary fuel tanks and was operationally more versatile since it could be employed in the transport rôle without requiring its tanker equipment to be removed.

Other designations, arising from the conversion of C–97 series aircraft for special purposes, were as follows:

C–97D Redesignation of seven aircraft—the third YC–97A, the YC–97B, two C–97As and the three VC–97Ds (see below)—after modification as passenger transports.
VC–97D Designation of three C–97As, converted for SAC as flying command posts with auxiliary underwing fuel tanks, upper-deck entry door on port side, and deletion of cargo doors. Later modified to C–97D standard.
C–97E Similar to KC–97E, but used as

Above: *A C–97G (KC–97G with refuelling equipment deleted) at Wellington Airport, New Zealand, in 1964.*

Below: *A KC–97L jet-boosted tanker of No. 181 Air Refueling Squadron of the Texas Air National Guard.* [via S. P. Peltz]

cargo, troop or passenger transport or for casualty evacuation. Crew of five.

C–97F As KC–97F, but has refuelling equipment removed and special installation to carry large engines, bulky mock-ups etc. Crew of four.

C–97G Cargo conversion (by deleting tanker equipment) of 135 KC–97Gs after transfer to Air National Guard.

HC–97G Search and rescue conversion from KC–97G by Fairchild-Stratos: 28 to Air Rescue Service in 1964.

KC–97H Conversion of one KC–97F to hose-refuelling tanker.

YC–97J Conversion of two KC–97Gs to a power plant of four 5,700ehp Pratt & Whitney YT34–P–5 turboprop engines. One later converted to Model 377–SG Super Guppy after becoming surplus to USAF requirements.

C–97K Conversion of 26 KC–97Gs to passenger transports for SAC Mission Support. Refuelling boom retained, but all other tanker equipment removed.

KC–97L Designation of an unknown number of ANG KC–97Gs after addition of two underwing J47 turbojet engines (from surplus KB–50s) to the standard power plant.

Israel Aircraft Industries acquired several C–97 series aircraft, including one of the original YC–97s, and to these were added five Stratocruisers (Model 377) purchased early in 1962. Various modifications, such as the provision of extra doors for paratroop dropping, were made to some of these aircraft, during which some interchange of Model 367 and 377 components almost certainly took place. From the combined batch, IAI later converted a number—up to a dozen, according to one report—to swing-tail cargo configuration for military use. In 1970, some C–97s were operating with the Israeli Air Force as two-point tankers for probe-and-drogue refuelling of its A–4 and F–4 aircraft.

Specification

SPAN	(YC–97)	141ft 3in
	(KC–97G)	141ft 3in
LENGTH	(YC–97)	110ft 4in
	(KC–97G)	117ft 5in
HEIGHT	(YC–97)	33ft 3in
	(KC–97G)	38ft 3in
WING AREA	(YC–97)	1,738sq ft
	(KC–97G)	1,769sq ft
GROSS WEIGHT	(YC–97)	120,000lb
	(KC–97G)	175,000lb
MAX SPEED	(YC–97)	346mph
	(KC–97G)	375mph
CRUISING SPEED	(KC–97G)	300mph
RANGE	(YC–97)	3,100 miles
	(KC–97G)	4,300 miles

Production

XC–97	43–27470 to 43–27472
YC–97	45–59587 to 45–59592
YC–97A	45–59593 to 45–59595
YC–97B	45–59596
C–97A	48–397 to 48–423
	49–2589 to 49–2611
C–97C	50–690 to 50–703
KC–97E	51–183 to 51–242
KC–97F	51–243 to 51–397
	51–7256 to 51–7259
KC–97G	51–7260 to 51–7271
	52–826 to 52–938
	52–2602 to 52–2806
	53–106 to 53–365
	53–3815 to 53–3816

Stratocruiser and 'Guppy' series
(Model 377)

THE 100-seat Stratocruiser was the commercial transport counterpart of the military Stratofreighter. Its configuration followed closely that of the YC–97B, and its prototype, which first flew on July 8, 1947, was in fact the next machine after this on the production line. A total of 55 other Stratocruisers was built, the first order (for 20) being placed in June 1946 by Pan American, with others following from SAS (four), American Overseas Airlines (eight), Northwest Airlines (ten), BOAC (six) and United Air Lines (seven). The first PanAm service was inaugurated on September 7, 1948.

As was to be expected in a descendant of the B–29, the Stratocruiser had an excellent range—well over 4,000 miles maximum—but it really made its mark with the unparalleled degree of passenger comfort which it offered. Like its military counterpart, it had a two-deck layout, and the nominal capacity of the accommodation was for up to 100 passengers in the main upper-deck cabin. In addition, there was a lounge on the lower deck, reached via a spiral staircase, which could accommodate a further 14 passengers. Interior layouts varied between individual airlines, but in practice this lounge was generally used as a bar or rest room where passengers could go to stretch their legs or refresh themselves during a long flight. The upper deck could be converted to a 'sleeper' configuration, offering bunks for 28 persons and seats for five others in addition to the standard washrooms and galley. The two lower cargo holds had a total volume of 900cu ft, and the flight crew consisted of five men.

At one time, Pan American had a total fleet of 27 Stratocruisers: its original 20, the prototype (acquired after completing its certification programme), and six of the AOA machines. All of these were later fitted with new turbo-superchargers, and 10 had additional tankage installed for non-stop services from New York to London or Paris. Most of the PAA aircraft were returned to Boeing in 1958–59 in part payment for its new fleet of Boeing 707s. One exception was NC1027V: this was sold to BOAC when the British airline urgently needed to plug the gap made in its services by the grounding of its Comet fleet in 1954. BOAC eventually operated 17 Stratocruisers: the six it had originally ordered, plus the four machines ordered by (but diverted before delivery to) SAS, six acquired from United Air Lines and the one from Pan American. After withdrawal from BOAC service in 1958, 14 were returned to Boeing, 10 being resold to Transocean Airlines; one had been lost in a crash, and the other two were sold for scrap in 1960. Ten other Stratocruisers were bought by RANSA of Venezuela, which operated three of them in a cargo capacity from 1961 until it went bankrupt in 1966. The Stratocruisers built originally for NWA and UAL could be distinguished by their rectangular, instead of circular, cabin windows.

Israel Aircraft Industries bought five Stratocruisers early in 1962: a note concerning these appears under the description of the C–97 Stratofreighter.

The 'Guppy' modifications

Some years after the Stratocruiser ceased to operate on regular airline services, it became the subject of one of the most bizarre modification programmes yet devised for any aeroplane. Many of the largest pieces of hardware for the US space programme—the Saturn launch vehicle in particular—are manufactured in the western United States, and their transportation to Cape Kennedy (then Cape Canaveral) by sea—the only practicable route—was both a lengthy and a costly undertaking. To produce an air vehicle capable of transporting these outsize loads more quickly and directly, Jack Conroy of Aero Spacelines Corporation acquired an ex-Pan American Stratocruiser (N1024V) and sent it, as a private venture, to the On Mark Engineering Company for modification in accordance with his own designs. As a first step, an additional 16ft 8in section from another Stratocruiser was inserted into the fuselage aft of the wings. Then a new and much larger upper fuselage structure was built, giving a 20-foot-high clearance on the upper deck. The aircraft was now large enough to accommodate Saturn rocket units, but there remained the problem of loading and unloading. This was accomplished by enabling the entire rear half of the aeroplane to be unbolted and moved away on its own special handling gantry. The gross appearance of the modified aircraft quickly earned it the nickname 'Pregnant Guppy'; the name stuck, and was later recognised officially when the conversion was given the revised Boeing Model number 377–PG. It flew for the first time on September 19, 1962. Since then, Aero Spacelines has acquired a

Boeing 377 Stratocruiser in the insignia of Pan American Airways.

number of ex-NWA Stratocruisers and USAF C–97s, from which it has developed variations on the 'Guppy' theme. Next to fly, on August 31, 1965, was the Model 377–SG Super Guppy (N1038V), rebuilt from one of the turboprop-engined YC–97Js, plus components from three other aircraft, and now powered by 7,000eshp T34–P–7WAs. This was even larger than its predecessor, having increased length and wing span, an upper-fuselage volume increased from 29,187cu ft to 49,790cu ft, and a hinged nose section (including the flight deck) for direct loading. Both aircraft were soon in operation under contract to NASA. For commercial loads such as the transportation of large aircraft sections, helicopters, oil-rig equipment etc, Aero Spacelines next developed the 377–MG Mini-Guppy (N1037V), which flew for the first time on May 24, 1967. This has R–4360–B6 piston-engines, the same overall wing span as the Super Guppy, and a fuselage 22ft 6in longer than the standard Stratocruiser with a hinged swing-tail fo cargo loading. The Guppy-101, a turbo-prop version of the Mini-Guppy, with swing-nose loading, was first flown on March 13, 1970, but was lost in a crash just after take-off for a subsequent flight on May 12. Latest version to be announced, up to late 1970, was the Guppy-201. This also has Allison 501–D22C turboprop engines and a swing-nose, is also the longest Guppy version to date (143ft 10in) and has a taller and more angular vertical tail. Its purpose is to air-lift large pre-assembled sections of the McDonnell Douglas DC–10 and wing assemblies of the Lockheed L–1011 TriStar airliners. In 1971, Aero Spacelines' plans were for an

The Stratocruisers of United and Northwest differed in having square cabin windows.　　[United Air Lines

A Stratocruiser in the markings of the Venezuelan operator RANSA.　　[Air-Britain

eventual mixed fleet of 10 or 12 Guppy-101 and Guppy-201 aircraft, in equal numbers. One Guppy-201 was used by UTA, under contract to Aérospatiale, to transport components of the A 300B European Airbus to the final assembly centre in France, starting in mid-1971.

Specification

SPAN	141ft 3in
LENGTH	110ft 4in
HEIGHT	38ft 3in
WING AREA	1,720sq ft
GROSS WEIGHT	148,000lb
MAX SPEED	375mph
CRUISING SPEED	340mph
RANGE	4,200 miles

Production

377–10–19	NX–90700
377–10–26	NC1023V to NC1042V
377–10–28	G–ALSA to G–ALSD
377–10–29	NC90941 to NC90948
377–10–30	NC74601 to NC74610
377–10–32	G–AKGH to G–AKGM
377–10–34	NC31225 to NC31231

Top: *Aero Spacelines'* 'Pregnant Guppy' *Stratocruiser conversion, taking off for its first flight on September 19, 1962.* [Aero Spacelines]

Left: *Front-loading swing-nose of the Guppy–101.* [Aero Spacelines]

Right: *With a top speed of 432mph and range of 3,500 miles, the XF8B–1 was a promising design, but only three prototypes were built.*

XF8B–1
(Model 400)

BOEING'S FIRST new 'F' design for nearly ten years, the XF8B–1 was actually in the 'attack' class, being a five-in-one design capable of operation as fighter, interceptor, attack aircraft, light bomber and torpedo bomber. The first of three prototypes was flown on November 27, 1944, and the XF8B–1 was extensively test flown by pilots of the US Navy, Marine Corps and Army during the next few years. The 10-ton fighter-bomber was the heaviest carrier-based US combat aircraft built during World War II, and potentially one of the most versatile. Design features included a fully-enclosed large-capacity bomb bay, heavy firepower with remote-control sighting, provision for the carriage of external weapons, and a 28-cylinder Wasp Major engine installed in a quick-change power package and driving two 13½ft Aeroprop three-blade contra-rotating propellers. As they retracted backward, the main landing gear units rotated through 90° to allow the wheels to lie flat in the wings—a feature licensed to Curtiss and

used in the P–36 and P–40 fighters, but hitherto unexploited by Boeing, who had developed it many years earlier. Construction of the XF8B–1, including the control surfaces, was entirely of metal.

The XF8B–1, designed specifically for long-range carrier-based strikes against Japan, had a range of 3,500 miles and a service ceiling comparable to that of the B–29. But when the B–29 brought the Pacific war more quickly to an end than expected, the need for the XF8B–1 vanished; this, and the rapid post-war evolution of jet-driven military aircraft, effectively halted the career of a promising aeroplane.

Specification

SPAN	54ft 0in
LENGTH	43ft 3in
HEIGHT	16ft 3in
WING AREA	489sq ft
GROSS WEIGHT	20,508lb
MAX SPEED	432mph
CRUISING SPEED	190mph
RANGE	3,500 miles

Production
57984 to 57986

B–47 Stratojet
(Model 450)

THE SHARING of preliminary information on jet propulsion during the early part of World War II, particularly after the flight in May 1941 of the first British jet aircraft, led the USAAF late in 1943 to issue to the American industry its initial outline requirements for jet bombers and reconnaissance aircraft. These were kept deliberately simple, the chief requisites being a 2,000-mile range and a maximum speed of 500mph at 40,000ft. Four competing bomber designs were ordered in prototype form: the North American XB–45, Convair XB–46, Boeing XB–47 and Martin XB–48. Of these, only the B–45 and B–47 subsequently entered production, the latter being produced in the greater numbers.

To meet the original USAAF requirement, Boeing first evolved a number of straight-winged designs, notably the Models 424 and 432, based on the B–29. Then, when the European war ended, company technicians were among those granted access to German aerodynamic research data, and a revised design, Model 450, was submitted late in 1945. It was the only one of the four competitors to utilise sweptback wings, and these were of such thin aerofoil section that all fuel and the novel bicycle landing gear, as well as the bomb load, had to be housed entirely within the fuselage. Another innovation was the installation of the power plant—two single and two pairs of 3,750lb st General Electric J35 turbojet engines—in underwing pods, with stabilising outrigger wheels retracting into the inboard pods. This—apart from the

Junkers Ju 287 in Germany—was the first application of swept wings to a large jet aircraft, and in conjunction with the podded underwing engine layout pioneered a configuration that was to become commonplace on commercial jet transports from the mid-1950s onwards. Built into the bomber's rear fuselage was a compartment for eighteen 1,000lb st JATO (Jet-Assisted Take-Off) solid-fuel rockets. Two 0·50in machine-guns in the tail, operable automatically or manually from the cockpit, constituted the only defensive armament, and the weapons bay had accommodation for normal and maximum bomb loads of 10,000lb and 22,000lb respectively. A three-man crew was carried, the pilot and co-pilot/gunner sitting in tandem seats beneath a fighter-style bubble canopy.

The first of two XB–47s was flown on December 17, 1947. The second, fitted with 5,200lb st J47–GE–3 engines (later installed also on the first machine), flew on July 21, 1948. The J47–GE–11, with the same rating, was installed on the ten B–47As which were then built, primarily for service testing. First major production version was the B–47B, of which 398 were completed, including eight by Lockheed and 10 by Douglas, who were to take a larger share of subsequent production. Most of these aircraft had 5,800lb st J47–GE–23 or –27 engines. One B–47B was earmarked for

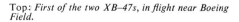

Top: *First of the two XB–47s, in flight near Boeing Field.*

Right: *Early-production B–47Bs, used for training with armament removed.*

conversion as a prototype reconnaissance aircraft with four Allison J71 engines: it was successively redesignated XB–56, YB–56 and finally YB–47C, but the conversion was never made and the proposed RB–56A production model was cancelled. Another testbed was the B–47B modified in 1956, by Canadair on behalf of the RCAF, to air-test the 20,000lb st Orenda Iroquois turbojet engine. Designated CL–52 by Canadair, this aircraft retained its normal power installation, the Iroquois engine being mounted in a separate pod at the rear of the fuselage on the starboard side.

The next production model to appear was the B–47E, first flown on January 30, 1953. More significant changes appeared in this, the most extensively-built model. Power plant was the 7,200lb st J47–GE–25; tail armament was two 20mm cannon; a more powerful (33-unit) jettisonable JATO pack replaced the built-in type on most aircraft; the nose section was re-designed to incorporate in-flight refuelling receiver gear and ejection seats for all three crew members; fuel capacity was reduced from 17,000 to 14,610 US gallons, including that in underwing drop-tanks; and the landing gear was strengthened to match the increased gross weight resulting from the other changes. Lockheed at Marietta, and Douglas at Tulsa, brought into the

Top: *Rocket-assisted take-off by a B–47E Stratojet.*

Centre: *Its longer, slimmer nose was a characteristic of the RB–47E photographic version.*

Right: *The ERB–47H nose, though elongated, was blunter.*

B–47 programme after the outbreak of the Korean war in 1950, built 286 and 264 B–47Es respectively; a further 691 were completed by Boeing at Wichita. Additionally, Boeing-Wichita built 240 RB–47E strategic reconnaissance models, differing from the B–47E by omitting the bombing capability, reverting to built-in JATO and having a battery of 11 cameras, slightly modified nose contours and an increased fuel capacity of 18,405 US gallons. Production of the B–47 series continued at Wichita with 35 RB–47H/ERB–47Hs: these were special radar-spotting reconnaissance aircraft carrying a crew of six and five respectively. The first RB–47H flew in June 1955. Final production model was the RB–47K reconnaissance-bomber, equipped also for weather reconnaissance. Fifteen of these, ordered originally as B–47Es, were built. Overall B–47 production thus totalled 1,941 aircraft: 1,373 by Boeing, 294 by Lockheed and 274 by Douglas. At the peak of its career with

Strategic Air Command, in 1957, there were some 1,800 Stratojets in service, and the B–47 remained a major type in the SAC inventory until 1966, when the bomber variants were withdrawn to the reserve. Last Stratojet variant in service, the WB–47E, was withdrawn in 1969.

One B–47E was used as a flying test-bed for the Pratt & Whitney TF34 turbofan engine, making its first flight with one of these engines in the port outer position on January 21, 1971.

There was a considerable variety of other B–47 designations, arising from conversions or special functions, as listed below:

B–47B–II Redesignation of B–47Bs brought up to B–47E standard: number not known.

DB–47B Unarmed director for QB–47E and other remote-controlled target aircraft: four converted from B–47B.

YDB–47B One DB–47B modified in 1953 as launch and director aircraft for Bell GAM–63 Rascal guided missile.

RB–47B Photographic reconnaissance aircraft, with eight cameras mounted in bomb bay: number of conversions not known.

TB–47B Pilot/navigator conversion trainer, with extra crew position for instructor: 66 converted from B–47B, 48 by Douglas and 18 by USAF.

WB–47B Weather reconnaissance, converted from B–47B: number not known.

XB–47D Unarmed flying testbed for Wright YT49–W–1 turboprop engine, one of which replaced each inboard pair of jet engines: two converted from B–47B.

YDB–47E For service trials with Rascal missile: two converted from B–47E.

DB–47E As YDB–47E: two converted from B–47E.

ETB–47E Special duty (electronics) trainer, converted from B–47E: number not known.

QB–47E Radio-controlled unmanned target drone: 14 converted from B–47E.

WB–47E Weather reconnaissance: 24 converted from B–47E.

YB–47F Fitted with probe for trials with KB–47G of probe-and-drogue refuelling system: one converted from B–47B.

KB–47G Hose-refuelling tanker for trials with YB–47F: one converted from B–47B.

YB–47J Test aircraft for MA–2 radar bombing and navigation system: one converted from B–47E.

EB–47L Electronic communications relay aircraft: 35 converted from B–47E in 1963.

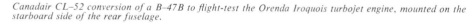

Canadair CL–52 conversion of a B–47B to flight-test the Orenda Iroquois turbojet engine, mounted on the starboard side of the rear fuselage.

Specification (B–47E–II)

SPAN	116ft 0in
LENGTH	109ft 10in
HEIGHT	27ft 11in
WING AREA	1,428sq ft
GROSS WEIGHT	206,700lb
MAX SPEED	606mph
COMBAT SPEED	557mph
RANGE	4,000 miles

Production

XB–47	46–65 to 46–66
B–47A	49–1900 to 49–1909
B–47B	49–2642 to 49–2646
	50–1 to 50–82
	51–2045 to 51–2356
B–47E–BW	51–2357 to 51–2445
	51–5214 to 51–5257
	51–7019 to 51–7083
	51–17368 to 51–17386
	52–394 to 52–620
	53–2261 to 53–2417
	53–4207 to 53–4244
	53–6193 to 53–6244
B–47E–LM	51–15804 to 51–15812
	52–202 to 52–393
	52–3343 to 52–3373
	53–1819 to 53–1972
B–47E–DT	52–19 to 52–120
	52–146 to 52–201
	52–1406 to 52–1417
	53–2028 to 53–2040
	53–2090 to 53–2170
RB–47E	51–5258 to 51–5276
	51–15821 to 51–15853
	52–685 to 52–825
	52–3374 to 52–3400
	53–4245 to 53–4264
RB–47H	53–4280 to 53–4309
	53–6245 to 53–6249
RB–47K	53–4265 to 53–4279

XL–15 and YL–15 Scout
(Model 451)

THE TWO-SEAT Scout light liaison and observation aircraft was developed by Boeing's Wichita Division. Keynote of the design was the provision of an outstanding all-round view for both crew members, and to obtain this a high-wing layout was adopted in association with a pod-and-boom fuselage, the high-mounted tailboom supporting the tailplane and dependent twin endplate fins and rudders. The front, sides, rear and roof of the cabin were extensively glazed in Plexiglas, giving almost complete all-round visibility. The wings were fitted with full-span, fully (and permanently) extended 'flaperons', capable of deflection between 10° up and 40° down from the normal zero setting and of operating differentially in conjunction with spoiler-type ailerons. To facilitate transit by road or air, the wings, and the entire tail assembly including the boom, could be quickly disassembled, and the main landing gear legs could be rotated inward to decrease the overall width.

The first of two XL–15 prototypes was flown on July 13, 1947. Tests were conducted with a twin-float gear as well as the original reverse-tricycle wheel gear, and in 1948–49 ten YL–15 aircraft were completed and delivered for service evaluation. These were basically similar to the XL–15 except for a slight increase in rudder area. Features of the design were its excellent STOL and slow-flying capabilities: it could take off and land over a 50ft obstacle in less than 600ft, fly at speeds down to 36mph, and be aero-towed, glider-fashion, behind a standard transport aircraft until released for a mission or landing under its own power. However, no Army production contract materialised, and in due course the YL–15s were handed over to the US Forest Service and the US Department of the Interior.

Specification

SPAN	40ft 0in
LENGTH	25ft 3in
HEIGHT	8ft 8½in
WING AREA	269sq ft
GROSS WEIGHT	2,050lb
MAX SPEED	112mph
CRUISING SPEED	101mph
RANGE	over 250 miles

Production

XL–15	46–520 to 46–521
YL–15	47–423 to 47–432

Second XL–15 Scout prototype, with twin-float landing gear.

B–52 Stratofortress
(Model 464)

THIS HUGE global bomber, which formed the spearhead of Strategic Air Command's nuclear deterrent force for a substantial part of the period since World War II, owed its origins to a USAAF specification issued in April 1945 for a long-range turbine-engined bomber. The state of knowledge at that time seemed to indicate that the range requirement could be met only by a turboprop-engined aeroplane, and the original application of the B–52 designation, in June 1946, was to a straight-winged Boeing design (Model 462) powered by six 5,500ehp Wright T35 turboprop engines. However, by the time two more years had elapsed the picture had changed considerably: it was obvious that in-flight refuelling was a pre-requisite of achieving the necessary range, whatever the type of power plant, and Boeing had by then flown the prototype of the shorter-range,

swept-wing turbojet-powered B–47. So, in October 1948, USAF approval was obtained to submit an entirely new design (Model 464) under the original designation. Much though the new project resembled a scaling up of the B–47 configuration, only the design principles remained the same. The Boeing 464 was an entirely new aeroplane. Power plant comprised eight 8,700lb st Pratt & Whitney YJ57–P–3 turbojet engines, paired in four pods under the sweptback wings. The box-section fuselage housed the five-man crew, four-unit tandem landing gear and most of the fuel load; and retractable outrigger wheels beneath the outer wing panels provided lateral stability on the ground. A tail turret with four 0·50in machine-guns, operable manually or automatically, constituted the defensive armament, and provision was made for an internal bomb load of 10,000lb.

The two B–52 prototypes ordered under the original 1946 contract thus materialised

as one XB–52 and one YB–52 to the Model 464 design. The latter was the first to fly, on April 15, 1952, followed on October 2 of that year by the XB–52. Nearly another two years elapsed before, on August 5, 1954, the first of three B–52A service test aircraft was flown. These had a crew of six, with escape systems for all members, and J57–P–9W engines. They also differed from the prototypes in having an airliner-style stepped windscreen, with a flight deck seating the two pilots side by side, instead of the bubble canopy over tandem seats that had characterised the two prototypes: this modification became standard on all subsequent production B–52s. Thirteen B–52As had been ordered originally, but the final 10 were completed (and redesignated) as B–52Bs. Total B–52B production, including these aircraft, amounted to 50 (23 B–52Bs and 27 RB–52Bs); they were powered by J57–P–19 or –29 series engines. Provision was made for a two-man pressurised camera or ECM

The XB–52 Stratofortress prototype, with Sabre 'chase' aircraft.

(Electronic Counter-Measures) capsule to be installed in the bomb bay, in which form the aircraft was designated RB–52B. The fuel load of 37,700 US gallons (including a 1,000 US gallon auxiliary tank under each outer wing panel) conferred on the Stratofortress a prodigious unrefuelled range, which could be further extended by in-flight refuelling. The bomber's capabilities in this direction were strikingly demonstrated in January 1957, when a trio of B–52Bs, flight-refuelled en route, carried out a non-stop round-the-world flight, completing the 24,325-mile journey in 45hr 19min at an average speed of 520mph.

By the use of 3,000-gallon auxiliary tanks the fuel load of the next version, the B–52C, was increased still further, and this, like the B–52B, had a dual bomber/reconnaissance capability. Thirty-five were built, followed by 170 bomber-only (but otherwise similar) B–52Ds. New and improved bombing, navigation and electronics systems were introduced in the B–52E (100 built), and only detail equipment changes from the E distinguished the B–52F, of which 89 were completed up to 1958.

The principal production model of the Stratofortress, and one which introduced a number of major modifications, was the B–52G. First flown on October 26, 1958, this was built exclusively at Wichita, where 193 were completed. Most noticeable external changes were the cropping of the vertical tail and replacement of the large underwing fuel tanks by smaller tanks holding only 700 US gallons each. To offset the latter alteration, internal tankage was increased to 46,000 US gallons. The tail armament was operated completely automatically from a position in the nose, causing a reshaping of the fuselage tail-cone. The operational effectiveness of the Stratofortress was extended in the B–52G by the ability to carry, on underwing pylons, two North American Hound Dog stand-off missiles, the 7,500lb st J52 engines of which could be used if necessary to boost the take-off power of the B–52G's own engines. Provision was also made to carry, in the bomb bay, two McDonnell Douglas Quail decoy missiles. Launched near a target, these can produce a 'B–52 image' on enemy radar screens to draw off intercepting fighters in a false direction.

Finally, Boeing built 102 examples of the B–52H, to bring overall Stratofortress production to 744, including prototypes. The B–52H, developed originally to carry the Douglas Skybolt nuclear stand-off missile (four, in pairs, on inboard wing pylons), was adapted to carry Hound Dogs or other weapons after the Skybolt programme was cancelled. It also featured the shorter, flat-topped fin of the G model, but was instantly recognisable from this and other Stratofortress variants by the shape and greater diameter of its engine nacelles, which housed four pairs of 17,000lb st Pratt & Whitney TF33–P–3

One of the three B–52Bs which took part in the 'Operation Power Flight' round-the-world flight in January 1957.

B-52D: a view which shows well the Strato-fortress's landing gear arrangement.

A B-52G in flight with Hound Dog missiles under the wings.

turbofans. One B–52H set up a new distance record for an unrefuelled flight when it flew 12,519 miles non-stop from Okinawa, in the south-west Pacific, to Madrid in January 1962.

Two Stratofortresses, a B–52A and an RB–52B, were allocated to NASA to act as launch-planes for the North American X–15 rocket-engined hypersonic research aircraft; after modification, these were re-designated NB–52A and NB–52B respectively.

The first B–52B was delivered to SAC in June 1955, and the last Stratofortress, a B–52H, in October 1962. Since that time it has been SAC's principal manned bomber; in 1970 a force of about 450 B–52s was still active, and current plans were for maintaining this strength for several more years. The B–52 force is capable of delivering a nuclear weapon at short notice to a target anywhere in the world, and a proportion of the force is kept constantly in the air to provide the USAF with a minimum 'reaction time' in the event of a surprise attack. More recently in its career, the B–52 has been employed for dropping leaflets or ordinary high-explosive or incendiary bombs on targets in Vietnam. All models from the D to H inclusive remained in service in 1971, the B–52D being among the aircraft operating against Vietnamese targets from bases in Thailand. At the culmination of its development, the B–52 was capable of carrying a total load of eighty-four 500lb bombs internally and twelve 750lb bombs on a pylon beneath each wing.

Specification (B-52G)

SPAN	185ft 0in
LENGTH	157ft 7in
HEIGHT	40ft 8in
WING AREA	4,000sq ft
GROSS WEIGHT	480,000lb
MAX SPEED	630mph
CRUISING SPEED	565mph
RANGE	12,500 miles

Production

XB–52	49–230
YB–52	49–231
B–52A	52–1 to 52–3
B–52B	53–373 to 53–376
	53–380 to 53–398
RB–52B	52–4 to 52–13
	52–8710 to 52–8716
	53–366 to 53–372
	53–377 to 53–379
B–52C	53–399 to 53–408
	54–2664 to 54–2688
B–52D	55–49 to 55–67
	55–68 to 55–117
	55–673 to 55–680
	56–580 to 56–630
	56–657 to 56–698
B–52E	56–631 to 56–656
	56–699 to 56–712
	57–14 to 57–29
	57–95 to 57–138
B–52F	57–30 to 57–73
	57–139 to 57–183
B–52G	57–6468 to 57–6520
	58–158 to 58–258
	59–2564 to 59–2602
B–52H	60–1 to 60–62
	61–1 to 61–40

The NB–52A used to air-launch the X–15 rocket-powered research aircraft.
[North American Rockwell Inc

Northrop HL–10 lifting-body re-entry vehicle beneath wing of the NB–52B 'mother' aircraft. The cut-out in the B–52's wing trailing-edge is to accommodate the tail fin of the X–15 when carried in this position.
[USAF

Model 367-80

AN ASSOCIATION of military bomber/commercial transport had already appeared three times in the first three decades of The Boeing Company's existence, with the B–9/Model 247, B–17/Stratoliner and B–29/Stratocruiser. So, having evolved two swept-wing bomber designs with podded underwing jet engines, it was probably inevitable that a transport aircraft of similar configuration should emerge sooner or later. However, the '707'—the aeroplane that even the most unairminded now know instantly by its Boeing Model number alone—did not begin its career as a direct development of either the B–47 or the B–52, even though it closely resembled the former in its ultimate configuration.

In 1950, after completing production of the Model 377 Stratocruiser, Boeing undertook a number of design studies, initially to develop a successor to the C–97 and employing turboprop or turbojet power. One such project was the Model 367-64, which envisaged a C–97-type fuselage fitted with moderately-swept wings which supported two pylon-mounted pairs of J57 turbojets. As the concept continued to develop, a new fuselage design was evolved and, for structural and safety

Top: *Historic moment: roll-out of the Boeing 367–80, prototype for the 707 transport.*

Right: *Extended nose section fitted to the 367–80 while testing a Bendix AN/AMQ–15 weather reconnaissance radar in 1959.*

reasons, the engines were arranged singly. By the time that the design was 'frozen' in 1952 as the Model 367–80 it no longer bore any relation whatsoever to the original Boeing 367; nevertheless, it was good business tactics to retain the 'Dash Eighty' designation as a piece of industrial 'camouflage', at least until a prototype was ready to be disclosed publicly.

The decision to proceed with a company-funded prototype was taken on May 20, 1952, and on May 14 two years later the aircraft was rolled out at Renton with a nation-wide wave of publicity. This now referred openly to the design as the Boeing 707, and the aircraft, registered N70700, made its first flight on July 15, 1954, powered by four 9,500lb st Pratt & Whitney JT3P turbojet engines. (It is, incidentally, a popular belief that this was the first flight by a jet transport designed in the United States: in fact it was antedated by more than three years by the experimental Chase XC–123A, which was flown with four J47 turbojet engines on April 21, 1951.)

At once it was clear that the Boeing 707's performance was considerably in advance of that of its closest rival, the de Havilland Comet, and it was to be another year before Douglas, Boeing's chief American competitor, decided to build a prototype jet airliner. But in purely marketing terms the 707 had appeared at a bad time. Clearly the airlines wanted, and eventually would have to have, jet transports in their fleets, but for the time being they had to recover in operating revenue some of the huge sums of money only recently invested in the latest versions of the major piston-engined transports. Thus they could not place immediately the firm orders which Boeing needed in order to start production of the 707. Fortunately, the designers of the 707 had always kept one eye on its application to military tanker/transport rôles, and it was in this form that the aircraft was first produced.

In the years since 1954 the 'Dash Eighty' prototype—still flying in 1971 and now known again firmly by its original designation—has served continuously as a test aircraft for a tremendous variety of features associated with the family of jet transports which has been developed from it. These features have included flying boom tanker gear, new power plants, new wing shapes and sections, high-lift flaps and slats, various boundary layer control systems, soft-field landing gear, weather radar, automatic landing equipment and many others, giving the 367–80 a 'modification record' probably unparalleled in commercial aviation history. The designation was amended to 367–80B after the aircraft was fitted with 17,000lb st JT3D–1 turbofan engines.

Separate descriptions of the military and commercial production models follow.

The 367–80 prototype while flight-testing a Boeing-designed blown-flap boundary layer control system and powered by turbofan engines which produce 28,000lb more in total thrust than the turbojets originally fitted to this aircraft.

KC–135 Stratotanker/
C–135 Stratolifter series
(Models 717 and 739)

AFTER its first flight in July 1954 the Boeing 367–80 prototype was evaluated by the United States Air Force both as a military transport and as a flight refuelling tanker. As a result the USAF placed an order in October 1954 for an initial quantity of 29 aircraft for the dual rôle, designated KC–135A and named Stratotanker. The first of these aircraft was flown on August 31, 1956. To distinguish it from the proposed commercial Model 707, the KC–135A was given the Boeing Model number 717. The new, highly-streamlined Flying Boom tested on the 'Dash Eighty' was installed, and the total fuel capacity of the KC–135A was 31,200 US gallons. This was carried in the wings and in the unpressurised lower portion of the fuselage; the pressurised upper shell could accommodate up to 80 passengers and some cargo. Power plant was four 13,750lb st Pratt & Whitney J57–P–59W turbojet engines. A total of 732 KC–135As was built, delivery of which to Strategic Air Command took place between June 1957 and January 1965. From the 583rd aircraft onward a taller fin and powered rudder were introduced, and this modification was also applied to the aircraft already

Top: *KC–135A Stratotankers of the 93rd Air Refueling Squadron, Strategic Air Command, at Castle AFB, California.*

Left: *KC–135A refuelling a General Dynamics (Convair) B–58 Hustler bomber.*

delivered. Another in-service modification was to adapt the nozzle of the refuelling boom to enable it to be used for probe-and-drogue refuelling as well. Four other aircraft were completed without refuelling booms and equipped with cameras: designated RC–135A, they are used by the Air Photographic and Charting Service of Military Airlift Command.

Next basic production version was the purely-transport C–135A Stratolifter, ordered for the Military Air Transport Service (now MAC) in 1961, which has a reinforced cabin floor and accommodation for 126 troops or 87,100lb of cargo. Of 45 ordered, only 15 were actually completed as C–135As. The remainder were built as C–135Bs (first flight February 12, 1962), with 18,000lb st TF33–P–5 turbofan engines and wider-span tailplanes. None of the 45 was completed with boom gear, but all retained provision for conversion to the tanker rôle if required. Three other 'partial' C–135As were converted from short-tailed KC–135A airframes; the first flight of a C–135A, on May 19, 1961, was made by one of these aircraft.

A new rôle, that of SAC Airborne Command Post, was allocated to 17 fan-engined KC–135Bs (later EC–135Cs), equipped with refuelling receptacles so that they could draw fuel from other tanker aircraft to extend their normal range. They carried a general officer with a 10-man staff

Top: *EC–135A 'flying command post', converted from an early production KC–135A.*
[Akira Hasegawa

Right: *NKC–135A special test aircraft.*

Above: *Turbofan-engined RC–135M (converted C–135B) at Yokota Air Base, Japan.*
[T. Matsuzaki

Left: *Boeing C–135F tanker of the French Air Force.* [Ministère des Armées 'Air'

in addition to a flight crew of five. Twelve C–135F (for France) tankers were delivered to the *Armée de l'Air*; these, like the KC–135As, have booms adaptable to provide probe-and-drogue refuelling for France's force of Dassault Mirage IV–A strategic bombers. Finally, 10 examples were built of the RC–135B, similar to the no-boom RC–135A but powered by TF33 turbofans and intended for electronics reconnaissance. Modifications to the RC–135A and RC–135B were such as to merit the new Boeing Model number 739 for these versions. Total production of the Models 717 and 739, which ended in 1966, amounted to 820 aircraft. Military VIP transports bearing VC–137 designations are variants of the commercial Model 707 and are listed under that heading. Some other 707s have been exported (*e.g.* to Canada and Germany) as military transports and/or tankers.

Special-function prefixes, and the allocation of new or revised series letters in 1965 to record structural or equipment changes, produced the following additional designations:

EC–135A Airborne command post/communications relay: six converted from KC–135A.

JKC–135A Special test aircraft for Systems Command, converted from KC–135A: number not known.

NKC–135A Special test aircraft for Systems Command, converted from KC–135A: number not known.

VC–135B VIP transport: 11 converted from C–135B.

WC–135B Weather reconnaissance: 10 converted from C–135B.

EC–135C Redesignation of 17 KC–135B in 1964. Three later to EC–135J.

RC–135C Electronic reconnaissance: 10 converted from RC–135B.

RC–135D Electronic reconnaissance: four converted from KC–135A, including deletion of boom.

RC–135E Electronic reconnaissance: one converted from C–135B.

EC–135G As EC–135A except internally: four converted from KC–135A.

EC–135H Airborne command post: five converted from KC–135A.

EC–135J Airborne command post: three converted from KC–135B/EC–135C.

EC–135K Airborne command post for TAC: one converted from KC–135A.

EC–135L Airborne command post/communications relay: three converted from KC–135A.

RC–135M Special mission conversion of C–135B.

EC–135N Airborne radio and telemetry relay station for Apollo space programme: eight converted by McDonnell Douglas from C–135A. Large nose radome.

EC–135P Airborne command post for Pacific Air Force: five converted from KC–135A.

KC–135Q Special KC–135A variant to refuel SR–71s with JP–7 fuel.

KC–135R Special reconnaissance version of KC–135A.

RC–135S Special reconnaissance version of RC–135D.

KC–135T Further modification of a KC–135R for ELINT collection.

Specification

SPAN	130ft 10in
LENGTH	136ft 3in
HEIGHT	38ft 4in
WING AREA	2,433sq ft
GROSS WEIGHT	297,000lb
MAX SPEED	600mph
CRUISING SPEED	552mph
RANGE	3,000 miles

Production

KC–135A	55–3118 to 55–3146
	56–3591 to 56–3658
	57–1418 to 57–1514
	57–2589 to 57–2609
	58–1 to 58–130
	59–1443 to 59–1523
	60–313 to 60–368
	61–261 to 61–325
	62–3497 to 62–3580
	63–7976 to 63–8045
	63–8871 to 63–8888
	64–14828 to 64–14840
C–135A	60–369 to 60–378
	61–326 to 61–330
C–135B	61–331 to 61–332
	61–2662 to 61–2674
	62–4125 to 62–4139
KC–135B	62–3581 to 62–3585
	63–8046 to 63–8057
C–135F	63–8470 to 63–8475
	63–12735 to 63–12740
RC–135A	63–8058 to 63–8061
RC–135B	63–9792
	64–14841 to 64–14849

Above: *Boeing 707–121 of Pan American Airways.*

Below: *Model 707–138 of Qantas, with spare engine in underwing pod.*

Models 707 and 720

As ALREADY EXPLAINED, the airline market situation at the time the Boeing 367–80 prototype appeared was such that immediate orders for the commercial Model 707 were not forthcoming. Happily for Boeing, there was no delay in selling its military counterpart to the USAF, and by keeping the initial commercial model essentially similar the company was able, with Air Force agreement, to utilise a certain amount of KC–135 tooling for production of the Model 707. The major basic difference was a 4in wider fuselage in the 707, though an entire family of 707 variants has since matured which incorporate various combinations of fuselage length, wing span, wing area and power plant. To improve directional stability, the height and area of the tail fin was increased in 1959: this modification became standard on all members of the 707/720 family built subsequently, and was made retrospectively to most of those already built. In addition to this feature, many aircraft also have an underfin beneath the tail-cone: this not only provides additional keel area but also serves as a tail bumper, acting as a safeguard against making a take-off run at too steep an angle.

The basic variants of the 707 family are identified by 'dash' numbers added to the Model number. These progress in increments of 100, the individual operator being identified by the last two digits of the dash number. Suffix letters B and C, added to the dash number, indicate respectively turbofan engines instead of turbojets, and turbofans plus cargo capability.

Above: *Model 707–328* Château de Versailles *in Air France livery.* [Air France

Below: *Boeing 707–347C transport of the Canadian Armed Forces.*

This system has been retained for identification of later Boeing jet transport designs as well; a table explaining the system and identifying operators by their dash numbers appears on pages 122 to 123.

707-120 and 720

The first 707 variant to go into production was the Model 707–120, of which the first example was flown on December 20, 1957. This 124/181-seat version was intended primarily for US domestic routes, but its range was sufficient to permit trans-Atlantic operation, and it was on the latter route that the 707–120 made its commercial debut. Pan American, which had ordered an initial batch of six, became involved in a somewhat undignified scramble with BOAC in the Autumn of 1958 to open the first jet service across the Atlantic. The British airline, naturally anxious to gain maximum operating advantage for its new fleet of Comet 4s, just 'won', though it is arguable whether any lasting benefit accrued from the achievement. Pan American's 707 service, from New York to Paris, began on October 26, 1958. US domestic 707 services were inaugurated on January 25, 1959, by American Airlines between New York and Los Angeles.

Standard power plant for the 707–120 is four 13,500lb st Pratt & Whitney JT3C–6 turbojets. Model number 707–220 was assigned to a similar version with the more powerful (15,800lb st) JT4A–3; in the event this was sold only to one airline, Braniff. A special short-fuselage version, 134ft 6in long, was produced specifically for Qantas as the 707–138: the original seven of these were later re-engined with turbofans as

–138Bs, and six more were built to the latter standard. Three 707–153s were purchased by the USAF for VIP transport duties. Their VC–137A designation became VC–137B after they too were converted to turbofan power. They seat 40 passengers, and serve with the 89th Military Airlift Wing, Special Missions, of MAC. Production of the –120 and –120B reached a total of 141 aircraft.

On November 23, 1959, Boeing flew the first example of a 110/165-seat 'baby 707'. Although bearing a close overall resemblance to the 707–120, this was sufficiently different structurally and dimensionally to justify the new Boeing Model number 720 (after being publicised initially as Model 717). The overall length was 7ft 9in shorter than the 707–120, but the main differences were to be found in the wing design, fuel capacity and operating weight. Whereas the leading-edge Krueger flaps of the –120 extended only to the outer engine location, they extended across almost the entire span of the 720, and the angle of leading-edge sweep was increased slightly between the inner engines and the fuselage. This version was built in a single size only, as the Model 720 with JT3C–7 (12,500lb st) or C–12 (13,000lb st) turbojets and as the Model 720B with JT3D–1 (17,000lb st) or D–3 (18,000lb st) turbofans. The first 720s to enter service were those of United Air Lines, on July 5, 1960; first flight of a 720B was made on October 6, 1960. Production of the 720/720B ended in 1969, a total of 154 having been completed. Dash numbers for the 720/720B are allocated in the –020 to –099 block, sometimes being applied as a Model 707 suffix.

The Model 707–120, when fitted with the turbofan power plant and improved wing features of the 720B, is known as the 707–120B.

Specification (707–120, –220, VC–137A)

SPAN	130ft 10in
LENGTH	144ft 6in
HEIGHT	42ft 0in
WING AREA	2,433sq ft
GROSS WEIGHT	257,000lb
MAX SPEED	623mph
CRUISING SPEED	549mph
RANGE WITH MAX PAYLOAD	3,217 miles

Production

367–80	N70700
707–121	N707PA to N712PA
707–123	N7501A to N7525A
707–123B	N7526A
	N7550A to N7554A
	N7570A to N7594A
707–124	N70773 to N70775
	N70785
	N74612
707–131	N731TW to N745TW
707–131B	N746TW to N752TW
	N754TW to N759TW
	N781TW to N785TW
	N795TW to N799TW
	N6720 to N6724
	N6726 to N6729
	N6763T to N6764T
	N6771T
	N6789T to N6790T
	N16738 to N16739
	N86740 to N86741
707–138	VH–EBA to VH–EBG
707–138B	VH–EBH to VH–EBM
707–139	N74613 to N74614

707–153	58–6970 to 58–6972
(VC–137A)	
707–227	N7071 to N7075

Specification (720B)

SPAN	130ft 10in
LENGTH	136ft 9in
HEIGHT	37ft 11in
WING AREA	2,433sq ft
GROSS WEIGHT	235,000lb
MAX SPEED	627mph
CRUISING SPEED	601mph
RANGE	4,155 miles

Production

720–022	N7201U to N7229U
720–023	N7527A to N7536A
720–023B	N7537A to N7551A
720–024B	N57201 to N57206
	N17207 to N17208
720–025	N8701E to N8715E
720–027	N7076 to N7080
	N113
720–030B	D–ABOH
	D–ABOK to D–ABON
	D–ABOP to D–ABOR
720–040B	AP–AMG to AP–AMH
	AP–AMJ
	AP–ATQ
720–047B	N93141 to N93153
	N3154 to N3167
720–048	EI–ALA to EI–ALC
720–051B	N721US to N737US
720–058B	4X–ABA to 4X–ABB
720–059B	HK–724 to HK–726
720–060B	ET–AAG to ET–AAH
	ET–ABP
720–062	N720V
	N720W
720–068B	HZ–ACA to HZ–ACB

707-320 and 707-420 Intercontinental

The first enlarged, long-range version of the 707, announced shortly after production of the 707–120 had started, was the Model 707–320 Intercontinental. Major features of this version are the use of 15,800lb st JT4A–3 or A–5 engines, with a substantial fuel increase, an 11ft 7in greater wing span and a 131/189-seat fuselage which increases the overall length by 8ft 5in compared with the –120. Uprated JT4A–9 (16,800lb st) or A–11 (17,500lb st) turbojets have been fitted in later production aircraft. First flight of a 707–320 was made on January 11, 1959, and this model entered airline service in the following August. A few operators—Air-India, BOAC, El Al, Lufthansa and Varig—opted for 17,500lb st Rolls-Royce Conway 508 turbofan engines in their aircraft, which thereby received the Model number 707–420. This version was first flown on May 20, 1959.

An improved Intercontinental, first ordered by Pan American and flown on January 31, 1962, is designated 707–320B and succeeded the original 707–320 in production. In addition to a turbofan power plant (18,000lb st JT3D–3s) this has a further-increased span with new low-drag wingtips, and new-style trailing-edge flaps of different shape and greater area. Later modifications include a revision of the leading-edge flaps, permitting deletion of the underfin at the tail if desired. The –320B entered airline service, with Pan

Top: *Boeing 707–436 of BOAC, with Rolls-Royce Conway engines.* [Alastair Macdonald

Right: *The aesthetically simple lines of the 707/720 series are well displayed in this fine view of a Lufthansa Model 720–030B.* [Lufthansa

American, in June 1962. One –320B (which retains the underfin) is the USAF's 49-passenger VC–137C, operated by the 89th Military Airlift Wing of MAC as the Presidential transport and for the carriage of other VIPs.

From the early 1960s a number of carriers have operated the 707–320C, a convertible cargo/passenger version retaining the essential features of the –320B but reinforced structurally and fitted with an 11ft 2in by 7ft 7in loading door in the port side of the forward fuselage. This version, which can accommodate 9,115cu ft of cargo or 215 passengers, entered service with Pan American in June 1963. An all-cargo, non-convertible version has up to 9,382cu ft of available cargo space. The Canadian Armed Forces and the Luftwaffe acquired five and four 707–320C transports respectively, and the Portuguese Air Force bought two; two of the Canadian aircraft were converted in 1970 to tanker/transports, with pods developed by Beechcraft beneath each wingtip containing hose-reels and drogues. The CAF designation for these aircraft is CC–137.

Total sales of the 707–320 and 707–420 had reached 561, of which 556 had been delivered, by April 30, 1971.

AWACS development

It was announced in July 1970 that Boeing had been selected as prime contractor and systems integrator for the US Air Force's AWACS (Airborne Warning And Control System) aircraft for service from the mid-1970s. Boeing's winning submission in this programme is based upon the Model 707–320 airframe, two of which were to be modified initially for com-parative trials with large (30ft diameter) rotating dorsal radomes designed by Hughes and Westinghouse. These aircraft have the customer dash number 707–3E3A, indicating their sale by Boeing's Commercial Airline Group to the company's Aerospace Group. Phase 2 was to involve a further five prototypes, each powered by eight General Electric TF34 turbofan engines mounted in pairs in underwing pods. These aircraft were to be used to evaluate fully the final airframe configuration, the avionics and the military equipment and systems. Initial production plans, if the first two phases were completed successfully, called for 42 aircraft, to be designated E–3A by the USAF.

Specification (707–320C, –420, VC–137C)

SPAN	145ft 9in
LENGTH	152ft 11in
HEIGHT	42ft 5in
WING AREA	3,010sq ft
GROSS WEIGHT	332,000lb
MAX SPEED	627mph
CRUISING SPEED	550mph
RANGE WITH MAX PAYLOAD	3,925 miles

Production and Sales (up to April 30, 1971)

707–307C	10–01 to 10–04
707–309C	B–1824 and B–1826
707–311C	CF–FAN
707–312B	9V–BBA to 9V–BBB
	9M–AOT
707–312C	Two for MSA
707–316C	CC–CEB
707–321	N714PA to N730PA
	N757PA to 759PA
707–321B	N760PA to N764PA
	N401PA to N410PA
	N412PA
	N414PA to N428PA
	N433PA to N435PA
	N453PA to N455PA
	N491PA to N497PA
	N880PA to N887PA
	N890PA to N897PA
707–321C	N765PA to N767PA
	N790PA to N799PA
	N445PA to N452PA
	N457PA to N463PA
	N473PA to N475PA
	N870PA to N872PA
	N17321 to N17322
707–323B	N8431 to N8440
707–323C	N7555A to N7569A
	N7595A to N7599A
	N8401 to N8406
	N8408 to N8417
707–324C	N17323 to N17329
	N47330 to N47332
	N67333
707–327C	N7095 to N7104
707–328	F–BHSA to F–BHSU
707–328B	F–BHSV
	F–BHSX to F–BHSZ
	F–BLCA to F–BLCB
	F–BLCD to F–BLCE
707–328C	F–BLCC
	F–BLCF to F–BLCL
707–329	OO–SJA to OO–SJG
707–329C	OO–SJH
	OO–SJJ to OO–SJO
707–330B	D–ABOT
	D–ABOV
	D–ABOX
	D–ABUB to D–ABUD
	D–ABUF to D–ABUH
	D–ABUK to D–ABUM

707-330C D-ABUA
D-ABUE
D-ABUI to D-ABUJ
D-ABUO
D-ABUY
707-331 N761TW to N772TW
N701PA to N706PA
707-331B N773TW to N780TW
N760TW
N793TW
N8705T
N8715T
N8725T
N18701 to N18704
N18706 to N18713
N28724
N28726 to N28728
N8729 to N8738
707-331C N786TW to N788TW
N791TW to N792TW
N1793T
N794TW
N5771T to N5774T
N15710 to N15713
707-336B G-AXXY to G-AXXZ
707-336C G-ASZF to G-ASZG
G-ATWV
G-AVPB
G-AXGW to G-AXGX
G-AYLT
707-337B VT-DPM
VT-DSI
VT-DVA
707-337C VT-DVB
VT-DXT
707-338C VH-EBN to VH-EBX
VH-EAA to VH-EAJ
707-340C AP-AUN to AP-AUO
AP-AVL, AP-AVZ
707-341C PP-VJR to PP-VJT
PP-VJH

707-344 ZS-CKC to ZS-CKE
707-344B ZS-DYL
ZS-EKV
707-344C ZS-EUW to ZS-EUX
ZS-FKT
ZS-SAH to ZS-SAI
707-345C N7321S to N7322S
PP-VJX
707-347C N1501W to N1505W
(Western)
707-347C 13701 to 13704 plus one more
(CAF)
707-348C EI-AMW
EI-ANO
EI-ANV
EI-APG
707-349C N322F to N325F
707-351B N351US to N355US
N377US to N381US
707-351C N356US to N376US
N382US to N386US
707-353B 62-6000
(VC-137C)
707-355C N525EJ and N527EJ
707-358B 4X-ATR to 4X-ATT
707-358C 4X-ATX to 4X-ATY
707-359B HK-1402 and HK-1410
707-360C ET-ACD
707-365C G-ATZD
N737AL
707-366C SU-AOU and SU-AOW
SU-APD to SU-APE
707-368C HZ-ACC to HZ-ACD
707-369C 9K-ACJ to 9K-ACL
707-372C N738AL to N739AL
707-373C N368WA to N376WA
N789TW to N790TW
707-379C N761U to N763U
(ET-ACQ, G-AWHU,
PP-VJK)
707-382B CS-TBA to CS-TBG

707-384B SX-DBE to SX-DBF
707-384C SX-DBA to SX-DBD
707-385C N8400
707-386C EP-IRL to EP-IRM
707-387B LV-ISA to LV-ISD
707-387C LV-JGP and LV-JGR
707-396C CF-ZYP
707-399C G-AVKA and G-AVTW
707-3B4C OD-AFB to OD-AFE
707-3D3C JY-ADO to JY-ADP
707-3E3A Two for Boeing Aerospace
(USAF prototypes)
707-3F5C Two for Portuguese Air Force
707-320C One for Korean Airlines
707-320C One for Nigeria Airways
707-430 D-ABOB to D-ABOD
D-ABOF to D-ABOG
707-436 G-APFB to G-APFP
G-ARRA to G-ARRC
707-437 VT-DJI to VT-DJK
VT-DMN
VT-DNY to VT-DNZ
707-441 PP-VJA to PP-VJB
PP-VJJ
707-458 4X-ATA to 4X-ATC
707-465 G-ARWD to G-ARWE

Dash numbers allocated to operators of Boeing jet transports

ALL AIRCRAFT in the Boeing jet transport family are identified by a 'dash number' following the basic Model number, which indicates both the sub-variant of the Model and the particular customer configuration. The sub-variant is indicated by a digit in the 'hundreds' position. In the case of the Boeing 707, four such variants have been produced and two others projected; the 727, 737 and 747 each existed in two basic sub-variants by 1971, with others being studied.

Following the 'hundreds' digit is a two-digit customer indicator. At first, Boeing began allocating numbers from 21 onwards to actual or potential airline customers for the Boeing 707. Thus, the first variant ordered (by Pan American) was the 707–121, in which the '21' was the Pan American designator and the '1**' indicated the original domestic variant of the 707. For reasons which are no longer clear, the 707 sub-variants were known as –120, –220, –320 and –420, rather than –100, –200 etc, and consequently '20' has not been used as a customer designator. Another exception to the system occurs in the case of the Boeing 720, which has no sub-variants; the customer number in this case is usually preceded by a '0' in the hundreds position, which can be regarded as a variant number in the 707 series.

Customer numbers, once allocated, remained effective for any of the Boeing jet transport types purchased by that airline. Thus, Pan American's Boeing 727s were 727–121s. Some numbers, allocated during negotiations which were not concluded with a sale, remained unused at the time of writing (early 1971). When all the numbers from 21 to 99 had been allocated, Boeing next used up the numbers from 1 to 19 and then continued with a letter/number combination: A0 to A9, then B0 to B9 and so on. These were used with the sub-variant 'hundreds' figures in exactly the same way as before. When aircraft pass from one customer to another in a second-hand deal, the original designator is retained.

As a further indication of configuration sub-variants, suffix letters are sometimes added after the customer designator. The suffix letter 'B' indicates turbofan engines in the Boeing 707–120 or 707–320 series only, while the letter 'C' indicates installation of a cargo-loading door and other provisions for cargo-carrying on any of the Boeing jet-liners. The suffix 'F' indicates an all-freight version, and so far has been applied only to the Boeing 747. (For a time, the second Boeing 747 sub-variant was identified by Boeing as the 747B, but for certification purposes this variant is now the 747–200.) The letters 'QC' as a suffix indicate 'quick change' capability between cargo and passenger configuration, but for certification purposes such aircraft carry only the 'C' suffix.

The table below lists, in sequence, dash numbers allocated up to the end of April 1971; second-hand deals are not shown, except in those cases where Boeing has sold aircraft of one airline configuration to a second customer.

01	Piedmont Airlines
02	Wien Air Alaska/Wien Consolidated Airlines
04	Britannia Airways
05	Braathens
06	KLM
07	German Federal Republic (Luftwaffe)
08	Icelandair
09	China Air Lines
10	Northern Consolidated/Wien Consolidated Airlines
11	Wardair
12	Malaysia-Singapore Airlines
13	Ariana Afghan Airlines
14	Pacific Southwest Airlines
15	Lake Central Airlines
16	LAN-Chile
17	CP Air
19	New Zealand National Airways
21	Pan American World Airways
22	United Air Lines
23	American Airlines
24	Continental Air Lines *and* Libyan Arab
25	Eastern Air Lines (Re-sales by Boeing to Korean Airlines, Calair, Trans-Polar and Voyager)
27	Braniff
28	Air France
29	Sabena
30	Lufthansa
31	Trans World Airways *and* Pan American (built for TWA)
32	Delta Air Lines
33	Air Canada
34	Transair Sweden
35	National Airlines
36	BOAC
37	Air-India
38	Qantas
39	Cubana (not delivered); Western Air Lines
40	Pakistan International Airlines
41	VARIG

42	Nordair
43	Alitalia
44	South African Airways
45	Seaboard World Airlines
46	Japan Air Lines
47	Western Air Lines *and* Canadian Armed Forces (built for WAL)
48	Aerlinte Eireann (Irish International)
49	Flying Tiger Line
51	Northwest Airlines
53	United States Air Force
55	Executive Jet Aviation
56	Iberia
57	Swissair
58	El Al
59	Avianca
60	Ethiopian Airlines
61	Federal Aviation Agency
62	Pacific Northern Airlines
63	Faucett
64	Mexicana
65	British Eagle/Cunard Eagle/BOAC
66	United Arab Airlines
68	Saudi Arabian Airlines
69	Kuwait Airways
71	Trans International
72	Riddle/Airlift International
73	World Airways
74	Mexicana
75	Pacific Western Airlines
76	Trans-Australia Airlines
77	Ansett Airlines of Australia
78	British West Indian Airways
79	Saturn Airways (not delivered); Ethiopian
80	TWA
81	All Nippon Airways
82	TAP
83	Scandinavian Airlines System
84	Olympic Airways
85	American Flyers

86	Iran Air (Iran National Airlines)
87	Aerolineas Argentinas
89	Japan Domestic Airlines
90	Alaska Airlines
91	Frontier Airlines
92	Air Asia *and* Southern Air Transport
93	Pacific Airlines (GATX–Boothe *and* Air California)
95	Northeast Airlines
96	Wardair
97	Aloha Airlines
99	Caledonian Airways
A0	Lloyd Aéreo Boliviano
A1	VASP
A3	PLUNA
A6	LTV *and* GATX–Boothe
A7	Trans Caribbean Airlines
A8	Indian Airlines
A9	Transair Sweden
B1	DETA
B2	Air Madagascar
B4	Middle East Airlines/Airliban
B6	Royal Air Maroc
B7	Allegheny Airlines
C0	GATX–Armco–Boothe
C3	Cruzeiro do Sul
D3	Alia Royal Jordanian Airlines
D5	Universal Airlines
D6	Air Algérie
E1	Eastern Provincial Airlines
E3	Boeing Aerospace
F5	Portuguese Air Force
H3	Tunis Air

Vertol Model 107/H–46 Sea Knight series

FIRST DESIGN STUDIES for this versatile twin-rotor helicopter were undertaken in 1956 by Vertol Aircraft Corporation (formerly Piasecki Helicopter Corporation). It was intended as a medium-size military or civil transport helicopter, powered by a pair of gas-turbine engines. A prototype of the design, known as the Vertol Model 107, was begun in May 1957, and this aircraft (N74060) flew for the first time on April 22, 1958, powered by two 860shp Lycoming T53 turboshaft engines. First interest in the Model 107 was shown by the US Army, which ordered 10 modified examples in July 1958 with the designation YHC–1A. The first of these (58–5514) was flown on August 27, 1959, by which time the Army had also ordered an evaluation batch of Vertol Model 114 helicopters as YHC–1Bs. This resulted in the YHC–1A order being reduced to three aircraft, of which the third was later fitted with 1,050shp General Electric T58–GE–6 engines and larger-diameter rotors to become the Model 107–II–1 commercial prototype.

US Army preference eventually favoured the YHC–1B Chinook (described separately), but in February 1961 a modified version of the YHC–1A was declared successful in a competition for a US Marine Corps medium assault/transport helicopter, and 14 production examples were ordered as the HRB–1 Sea Knight. By this time Vertol had become (in March 1960) a Division of The Boeing Company: hence the Sea Knight's company desig-

nation was Boeing-Vertol 107M. Its military designation was changed to CH–46A from July 1962. The T58-engined YHC–1A (later redesignated CH–46C) was flown on October 25, 1960, and was followed on May 19, 1961, by a new commercial 107–II prototype built to the requirements of New York Airways. This had 1,250shp CT58–110–1 engines, taller rotor pylons and square cabin windows. Five more, designated 107–II–10, were ordered by NYA, which put the type into regular passenger service on July 1, 1962.

The first CH–46A was flown on October 16, 1962, and delivery had been made to five USMC squadrons by the Summer of 1965. Repeat orders continued to be placed, these being delivered from September 1966 as CH–46Ds or UH–46Ds, with 1,400shp T58–GE–10 engines replacing the 1,250shp T58–GE–8Bs and larger rotors with cambered blades. Further-developed versions, designated CH–46E and CH–46F, were scheduled for procurement in 1971. Normal accommodation in the CH–46 is for a flight crew of three and 17–25 troops or 15 stretchers and two medical attendants. This model, which has power-folding rotor blades and a rear loading ramp, has served as an assault or logistics transport with the USMC in the Atlantic, Pacific and Mediterranean areas and in Vietnam. The US Navy, which has Sea Knights aboard its Fast Combat Support Ships, uses the UH–46A and UH–46D for 'vertical replenishment'

Top: *Vertol-built YHC–1 (Model 107) prototype.*

Left: *Vertol 107–II, production model for NYA, with square cabin windows.*

of supplies to combat vessels at sea. First UH–46A was delivered in June 1964, to Squadron VHU–1. Total CH–46/UH–46 orders are undisclosed, but the 500th aircraft of this type was delivered in June 1969 and production was continuing in 1971. The designation RH–46A covers a small number of aircraft converted for mine-hunting and mine-sweeping.

Exported US–built military models have included 18 for the Canadian Armed Forces (six 107–II–9s to the Air Force as CH–113 Labradors for search and rescue or transport duties, twelve to the Navy as CH–113A Voyageur cargo transports); and 13 Gnome-engined aircraft, designated HKP 4, to Sweden (ten 107–II–14s to the Army for search and rescue, three 107–II–15s to the Navy for anti-submarine patrol and mine-sweeping). Since June 1965, exclusive rights to build and market all civil models of the 107–II, and all military versions except those for the US and Canada, have been vested in Kawasaki of Japan. This company builds the helicopter under a basic KV–107/II designation, for which FAA type approval was granted in November 1965. Japanese versions announced up to the end of March 1971 were as follows:

KV–107/II–1 Basic utility version: none yet built.
KV–107/II–2 25-seat airline version. Built for Air Lift Inc of Japan (two), Pan

Top: *Kawasaki-built KV–107/II–5 of the Japan Air Self-Defence Force.*

Right: *UH–46A utility version of the Sea Knight, in service with the US Navy's Atlantic Fleet.*
[US Navy

American (three, for operation by New York Airways) and Thailand (three), plus two for company test.

KV–107/II–3 Mine countermeasures version, similar to RH–46A, with extra fuel, towing winch and cargo sling: two built, of initial order for four, for JMSDF.

KV–107/II–4 Troop/cargo transport version, with strengthened floor: 30 built, of initial order for 42, for JGSDF.

KV–107/II–5 Long-range search and rescue version, with rescue hoist, searchlights and auxiliary fuel tanks on cabin sides: 15 built, of initial order for 17, for JASDF.

KV–107/II–6 De luxe transport version: none yet built.

KV–107/II–7 6/11-seat de luxe transport version: one built, for Thailand.

KV–107/IIA Improved 'hot and high' model, with 1,500shp CT58–140–1 engines: one demonstrator built, first flown April 3, 1968.

Specification

ROTOR DIAMETER	(107–II)	50ft 0in
(each)	(CH–46D)	51ft 0in
FUSELAGE	(107–II)	83ft 4in
LENGTH	(CH–46D)	84ft 4in
HEIGHT		16ft 8½in
ROTOR DISC	(107–II)	1,962sq ft
AREA (each)	(CH–46D)	2,043sq ft
GROSS WEIGHT	(107–II)	19,000lb
	(CH–46D)	23,000lb
MAX SPEED	(107–II)	168mph
	(CH–46D)	166mph
CRUISING SPEED	(107–II)	150mph
	(CH–46D)	154mph
RANGE	(107–II)	110–630 miles
	(CH–46D)	230 miles

Production

107	N74060
YHC–1A (CH–46C)	58–5514 to 58–5516
107–II (107–II–10)	N6672D to N6676D
HKP 4 (107–II–14)	04 061 to 04 063
HKP 4 (107–II–15)	04 451 to 04 460
CH–113 (107–II–9)	10401 to 10406
CH–113A	10407 to 10418
KV–107/II–2	Three for Thailand
	Two for Air Lift Inc
	Three for PAA/NYA
	Two for Kawasaki
KV–107/II–3	Four for JMSDF
KV–107/II–4	Forty-two for JGSDF
KV–107/II–5	Seventeen for JASDF
KV–107/II–7	One for Thailand
KV–107/IIA	One for Kawasaki
CH–46A	
RH–46A	
UH–46A	
CH–46D	Quantities and serial numbers restricted
UH–46D	
CH–46E	
CH–46F	

CH–47 Chinook
(Vertol Model 114)

A YEAR BEFORE it became a Division of Boeing, Vertol Aircraft Corporation was announced the winner, over four other competitors, in a US Army design competition for a 'battlefield mobility' helicopter capable of lifting a 2-ton internal or 8-ton external load. Three months later, in June 1959, a contract was placed for five service test examples of this design, the Vertol Model 114, under the designation YHC–1B Chinook. The YHC–1A designation was meanwhile allotted to three prototypes of the smaller Vertol 107 (which see), also purchased for Army evaluation. First flight of a YHC–1B was made on September 21, 1961, by the second aircraft (59–4983), the first having been allocated earlier in the year for ground resonance testing. Three production batches of 5, 18 and 24 HC–1Bs had been ordered by the end of 1961, and with the adoption of a new tri-service designation system in 1962 the aircraft became known as the CH–47A. Deliveries began in December 1962, and the Chinook became fully operational with the US Army's First Cavalry Division (Air Mobile)—formerly the 11th Air Assault Division—in 1963.

The CH–47A's large, watertight fuselage is capable of transporting up to 44 armed troops, 24 stretchers with two medical attendants, or a maximum payload of 10,336lb, including vehicles and components of the Army's Pershing missile system. Prototypes and early production aircraft were powered by two 2,200shp Lycoming T55–L–5 turboshaft engines, each driving a three-blade rotor, but on

later aircraft these were replaced by the 2,650shp T55–L–7 model of the same engine. From 1965, when the Chinook began to be deployed extensively in Vietnam, output of the helicopter was increased and accelerated, and an 'armed and armoured' version made its appearance. This was intended to provide fire support for airborne operations and had more than 2,000lb of built-in or bolt-on armour protection. Armament included an M–5 40mm automatic grenade launcher beneath the nose, five 7·62mm or 0·50in machine-guns in the main cabin (two each side and one mounted on the rear loading ramp to fire aft), and an external mount on each side of the cabin for a 20mm cannon and either a 7·62mm Gatling gun or a $19 \times 2·75$in rocket pod. Four examples were evaluated, but this version of the Chinook was not adopted operationally.

A heavier and more powerful version appeared in October 1966, when the first of two YHC–47B prototypes was flown for the first time. This model is powered by 2,850shp T55–L–7C engines, driving slightly larger rotors with cambered blades, and can lift a 14,550lb payload. Deliveries of production CH–47Bs began in May 1967, followed in the Spring of 1968 by the CH–47C (first flown on October 14, 1967), which has 3,750shp T55–L–11 engines and still higher operating weights. Official production quantities for Chinook variants have not been disclosed, but a total of 550 had been delivered by February 1969, approximately half of which had been

Early production CH–47A Chinook, transporting a damaged Bell UH–1 helicopter to a repair base in south-east Asia.

127

deployed in the campaigns in south-east Asia. US production was still continuing at the end of 1970. In mid-1970 the RAAF placed an order for 12 CH–47Cs, and in September of that year 16 ex-US Army Chinooks were transferred to the Vietnamese Air Force. Elicotteri Meridionali of Italy has a Boeing licence to co-manufacture the CH–47C version for customers in Austria, Italy, the Middle East and Switzerland. Initial Italian production, which began in the Spring of 1970, was to fulfil orders from the Italian Army (26)

and the Iranian Air Force (16); the first eight aircraft (four for each customer) were built by Boeing-Vertol.

On May 27, 1970, Boeing flew the prototype of a CH–47A derivative known as the Boeing-Vertol Model 347. This is a research aircraft, Army-sponsored but company-funded. It has a 9ft 2in longer fuselage, four-blade rotors of increased diameter (61ft 7$\frac{1}{4}$in) and retractable landing gear in its initial form; provision has been made for the addition of wings at a later development stage.

Specification (CH–47C)

ROTOR	
DIAMETER (each)	60ft 0in
FUSELAGE	
LENGTH	99ft 0in
HEIGHT	18ft 7in
ROTOR DISC AREA (each)	2,826sq ft
GROSS WEIGHT	46,000lb
MAX SPEED	190mph
CRUISING SPEED	137mph
RANGE	50–230 miles

Production (Boeing production only)
Complete details classified. Known USAF serial numbers include the following:

YCH–47A	59–4982 to 59–4986
CH–47A	59–3448 to 59–3452
	61–2408 to 61–2425
	62–2114 to 62–2132
	63–7907 to 63–7918
	64–13106 to 64–13158
	65–7987 to 65–8024
	66–074 to 66–101
CH–47B	66–19075 to 66–19102
	67–18439
CH–47C	67–18494 to 67–18496
	67–18517 to 67–18542
	68–15810 to 68–15865
	Four for Imperial Iranian Air Force
	Four for Italian Air Force
	Twelve for RAAF
Model 347	65–7982 (cvtd from CH–47A)

Top: *CH–47C version of the Chinook twin-turbine helicopter.*

Left: *Prototype of the long-bodied Boeing-Vertol 347, first flown in 1970.*

Model 727

WITH THE 707/720 series of jet transports suited primarily to medium-to-long range operation, it was clear that there was room in the family for other aircraft intended for intermediate- and short-range services. To fulfil the former of these requirements Boeing began to pursue design studies in mid-1956, some two years before the initial model of the 707 entered airline service. Nearly nine years were to elapse before the outcome of these studies, the Model 727, was flown for the first time. During that period some 150 different design studies were undertaken, of which 68 were actually tunnel-tested, before the final configuration was settled in September 1960. Boeing designers followed a logical inclination to retain as many 707/720 features and components as were consistent with the requirements for the new type, but having decided upon three engines as the optimum number for reasons of economy, safety and performance a major change in the basic configuration became inevitable, resulting in the grouping of the engines at the rear of the fuselage instead of the more traditional Boeing underwing arrangement. From the cabin floor upwards, the fuselage cross-section of the 727 is identical with that of the 707, and the two aircraft have many other systems and components in common. Excellent take-off and landing characteristics are achieved by a system of wing lift devices and other control surfaces first tested thoroughly on the 'Dash Eighty' prototype. These include retractable slats on the outer leading-edges, with Krueger flaps on the inner sections; new, triple-slotted flaps on the trailing-edges; high- and low-speed ailerons; and both flight and ground spoilers.

No separate prototype of the 727 was built, the first flight on February 9, 1963, being made by a production aircraft, of which United Air Lines and Eastern Air Lines had each ordered 40. The Model 727 originated as an 88/119-seat transport, carrying a flight crew of three and intended for operation over routes from 150 to 1,700 miles in length. Power plant was three 14,000lb st Pratt & Whitney JT8D–1 turbofan engines. The aircraft entered airline service on February 1, 1964, with Eastern; United's services began four days later. Later aircraft have JT8D–7 (14,000lb st) or D–9 (14,500lb st) engines and seating for up to 131 passengers.

It had been found that the original 727 was capable of carrying its normal load over stage lengths of up to 2,500 miles—much farther than the distance first planned—and hence it was obviously possible, over the shorter distance, for the aircraft to carry a greater load. Thus, in August 1965, Boeing announced a stretched version of the design, with a 20ft longer fuselage seating up to 189 passengers. This became known as the 727–200, the distinguishing series number –100 being applied retrospectively to the original model. Construction of the 727–200 began in September 1966, and the first aircraft was flown on July 27, 1967. The first –200 customer, Northeast Airlines, placed the type in service that December. Standard engine is the JT8D–7, but some 727–200s have the JT8D–9 or the 15,000lb st JT8D–11.

As with the 707 series, a convertible cargo/passenger version of the 727 was offered in mid-1964, in the form of the 727C (later 727–100C), having JT8D–7 or D–9 engines, a large loading door forward and accommodation for a maximum of 131 passengers or 44,000lb of cargo. Even more popular, however, has been the QC (Quick Change) model, conversion of which from passenger to freight configuration can be accomplished by the operator in a considerably shorter time. Complete changeover of a 727–100QC, in either direction, can be made in less than an hour, compared with the several hours necessary for the 727–100C version.

In 1971 Boeing introduced the Advanced 727, which is essentially the 727–200 with a more luxurious interior, increased fuel, JT8D–9, –11, or –15 engines and a maximum ramp weight of 191,000 lb.

By the end of 1970 the Boeing 727 had surpassed the sales total of the 707 family to become the world's largest-selling (as well as fastest-selling) jet airliner. A total of 873 had been ordered by April 30, 1971, of which 847 had been delivered.

Specification

SPAN		108ft 0in
LENGTH	(–100)	133ft 2in
	(–200)	153ft 2in
HEIGHT		34ft 0in
WING AREA		1,700sq ft
GROSS WEIGHT	(–100)	169,000lb
	(–200)	175,000lb
MAX SPEED		630mph
CRUISING SPEED	(–100)	570mph
	(–200)	568mph
RANGE with max payload	(–100)	1,900 miles
	(–200)	1,290 miles

Production and Sales (up to April 30, 1971)
Boeing 727-100 Series

727–108C	TF–FIE
	plus one more
727–109	B–1818 and B–1820
727–109C	B–1822
727–111	CF–FUN
727–113C	YA–FAR and YA–FAU
727–114	N970PS to N977PS
727–116	CC–CAG and CC–CAQ
727–116C	CC–CFD to CC–CFE
727–117	CF–CPK and CF–CPN
	plus two more
727–121	N314PA to N321PA
	N323PA to N329PA
	N355PA to N360PA
727–121C	N339PA to N342PA
	N388PA to N389PA
727–122	N7001U to N7042U
	N7044U to N7050U
	N7052U to N7090U
727–122C	N7401U to N7438U
727–122	N68650
727–123	N1970 to N1998
	N1901 to N1903
	N1905 to N1910
	N1928 to N1935
	N1955 to N1956
	N1964 to N1965
	N1969
	N2913 to N2914
727–124C	N2475
727–125	N8101N to N8150N
727–125C	N8151G to N8175G
727–127	N7289 to N7290
	N7292 to N7294

Top: *First Boeing 727–100 in prototype/demonstration livery.*

Centre: *Boeing 727–122 of United Air Lines.*

Right: *Model 727–2B6 of Royal Air Maroc.*

727–127C	N7270 to N7281
	N7287 to N7288
	N7295 to N7296
727–129	OO–STA to OO–STC
727–129C	OO–STB
	OO–STD and OO–STE
727–130	D–ABIB to D–ABID
	D–ABIF to D–ABIH
	D–ABIK to D–ABIN
	D–ABIP to D–ABIT
	D–ABIV
727–130C	D–ABIA, D–ABIE
	D–ABII, D–ABIJ, D–ABIO
	D–ABIU
	D–ABIW to D–ABIZ
	D–ABBI
727–131	N831TW, N833TW
	N839TW to N842TW
	N844TW to N859TW
	N889TW
	N7890, N97891
	N7892 to N7893
727–131C	N890TW to N895TW
727–134	SE–DDA to SE–DDB
727–134C	SE–DDC
727–135 (National)	N4610 to N4622
727–135 (American)	N1957 to N1959
727–141	PP–VLD
	PP–VLF to PP–VLH
727–144	ZS–DYM to ZS–DYP
	ZS–DYR and ZS–EKW
727–144C	ZS–EKX
	ZS–SBH and ZS–SBT
727–146	JA8307 to JA8312
	JA8318 to JA8320
	JA8325 to JA8327
727–151	N461US to N480US
727–151C	N488US to N499US
727–155C	N530EJ to N531EJ

727–159	HK–727, HK–1337
	HK–1400 to HK–1401
727–161	N127
727–162	N7271P
727–162C	N2727 and N3727
727–163	OB–R–902
727–164	XA–SEJ
	XA–SEL to XA–SEM
727–171C	N1727T and N1728T
727–172C	N725AL to N727AL
	N732AL
727–173C	N690WA to N695WA
727–176	VH–TJA to VH–TJF
727–177	VH–RMD to VH–RMF
	VH–RMR
727–177C	VH–RMS to VH–RMT
727–178	9Y–TCO to 9Y–TCQ
727–180C	N9515T to N9516T
727–181	JA8301 to JA8303
	JA8305 to JA8306
	JA8316 to JA8317
	JA8321
727–182	CS–TBK to CS–TBM
	plus one more
727–182C	CS–TBN to CS–TBO
727–185C	N12826 to N12827
727–186	EP–IRA to EP–IRD
727–189	JA8314 to JA8315
727–190C	N766AS
	N797AS to N798AS
727–191	N7270F to N7274F
727–192C	N5055, N5092 to N5093
727–193	N898PC
	N2969G and N2979G
727–195 (Northeast)	N1631 to N1638
727–195 (American)	N1962 to N1963
727–1A7C	N8789R
727–1A0	CP861
727–1C3	PP–CJE to PP–CJG

Boeing 727-200 Series

727–214	N528PS to N545PS
727–222	N7620U to N7647U
727–223	N6800 to N6839
	N6841
727–224	N88701 to N88715
727–224 (Continental)	N32716 to N32719
727–224 (Libyan Arab)	5A–DAH to 5A–DAI
727–225	N8825E to N8850E
727–227	N401BN to N403BN
727–228	F–BOJA to F–BOJF
	F–BPJG to F–BPJQ
	plus three more
727–230	D–ABCI, D–ABDI
	plus three more
727–231	N12301 to N12308
	N52309 to N52313
	N94314, N64315, N44316
	N74317 to N74318
	N64319 to N64324
	N54325 to N54335
727–235	N4730 to N4754
727–247	N2801W to N2806W
727–251	N251US to N274US
727–254	N547PS to N549PS
	N384PS, N536PS
727–274	XA–TAA to XA–TAC
727–281	Eight for All Nippon
727–284	SX–CBA to SX–CBE
727–291 (Frontier)	N7276F to N7278F
727–291 (Northeast)	N1648 to N1649
727–295	N1639 to N1647
	N1650 to N1651
727–2A7	N8790R to N8791R
727–2B6	CN–CCF plus one more
727–2B7	N750VJ to N751VJ
727–2D6	7T–VEA to 7T–VEB
727–2H3	One for Tunis Air

Model 737

THE SHORT-HAUL MEMBER, and real baby, of the Boeing jet transport family is the Model 737. First announced in February 1965, this is an 80/115-seat aircraft, continuing the policy of structural commonality with the 707/720/727 series. The fuselage is noticeably shorter than either the 707 or 727, the retention of a common upper-fuselage diameter thus producing much tubbier proportions than those of other Boeing transports. The Model 737 utilises a similar system of wing lift and control surfaces to that of the 727, though the planform is somewhat different. Power, as in several of the 727 models, is provided by the 14,000lb st JT8D-7 turbofan, two of which are mounted in nacelles attached to the wing undersurface, instead of on pylons as in the 707 series. The uprated D-9 version of this engine is available optionally.

The initial version of the 737, first ordered by Lufthansa (21), was flown on April 9, 1967. This model is designated 737-100 and entered service on February 10, 1968. Following the precedent of the 727 a stretched version, the 737-200, soon followed, with the same power plant, a 6ft 4in longer fuselage and accommodation increased to a maximum of 125. First flight of a -200 took place on August 18, 1967, and this version entered service with United (who had ordered 40) on April 28,

Top: *Boeing 737-100 prototype.*

Right: *Model 737-2A9C of Transair; this is a rough-field version, with protected nose-wheel and 'blow-away' jets on the main nacelles.*

1968. Convertible and quick-change versions of the –200 are available as the 737–200C and 737–200QC respectively, the QC using the same standard-size cargo pallets as all other Boeing jet transports. Cargo capacity is 34,270lb. First customer for the –200QC was Wien Consolidated Airlines. A fifth basic version, known as the 737–200 Business Jet, is a longer-range model with a custom-styled luxury interior. Model 737 production-line improvements in 1969–70 included more efficient thrust reversers and drag-reducing refinements to improve the range. These are also available as conversion kits for aircraft already in service.

As a contender in the short-haul market, the Boeing 737 was a rather late starter, the design being announced only three days before the first flight of one major rival (the DC-9) and only some six weeks before another (the BAC One-Eleven) actually entered airline service. Problems met during the test programme also caused a slight delay before initial deliveries began. Early on, Boeing's estimated break-even figure for the 737 was 350 aircraft: by April 30, 1971, a total of 278 had been ordered, of which 267 had been delivered. Prospects of achieving the initial target figure should be enhanced by the intention to introduce, from mid-1971, short-field 'Advanced' versions of the –200, –200C/QC and –200 Business Jet. These were to have an improved high-lift system, better braking and, optionally, 15,500lb st JT8D–15 turbofan engines, features which would enable the aircraft to operate from 4,000ft instead of 5,000ft runways. The earlier models are already FAA-certificated to operate from unpaved or gravel strips.

Specification

SPAN	93ft 0in
LENGTH	(–100) 94ft 0in
	(–200) 100ft 0in
HEIGHT	37ft 0in
WING AREA	980sq ft
GROSS WEIGHT	(–100) 110,000lb
	(–200) 114,500lb
MAX SPEED	586mph
CRUISING SPEED	529mph
RANGE with max	(–100) 1,840 miles
payload	(–200) 2,135 miles

Production and Sales (up to April 30, 1971)

Boeing 737-100 Series

737–112	9M–AOU to 9M–AOW
	9V–BBC and 9V–BBE
737–130	D–ABEA to D–ABED
	D–ABEF to D–ABEI
	D–ABEK to D–ABEW
	D–ABEY
737–159	HK–1403 to HK–1404

Boeing 737-200 Series

737–201	N734N to N738N
	N740N to N741N
	N743N to N747N
737–202	N2711R
737–204	G–AVRL to G–AVRO
	G–AWSY and G–AXNC
737–204C	G–AXNA to G–AXNB
737–205	LN–SUP and LN–SUS
737–205C	LN–SUA
737–210C	N4902W
	N4906 to N4907
737–212	One for MSA
737–214	N378PS to N382PS
	N983PS to N989PS
737–217	CF–CPB to CF–CPE
	CF–CPU to CF–CPV
	CF–CPZ
737–219	ZK–NAC to ZK–NAE
737–222	N9001U to N9075U
737–230C	D–ABBE, D–ABCE
	D–ABDE, D–ABFE
	D–ABGE, D–ABHE
737–242C	CF–NAB, CF–NAH
	CF–NAQ
737–244	ZS–SBL to ZS–SBP
	ZS–SBR
737–247	N4501W to N4530W
737–248	EI–ASA to EI–ASB
	EI–ASF to EI–ASH
737–248C	EI–ASC to EI–ASE
737–253	19 for USAF
737–275	CF–PWC to CF–PWD
737–275C	CF–PWE
737–281	JA8401 to JA8403
	JA8405 to JA8411
	plus three more
737–286	Two for Iran Air
737–286C	Two for Iran Air
737–287	LV–JMW to LV–JMZ
737–287C	LV–JND to LV–JNE
737–291	N7373F to N7377F
737–293	N468AC to N470AC
	N831PC to N836PC
737–297	N73711 to N73715
737–297C	N73717
737–2A1	PP–SMA to PP–SME
737–2A3	CX–BHM
737–2A6	N502L
	N1288
737–2A8	VT–EAG to VT–EAM
737–2A9C	CF–TAN to CF–TAO
737–2B1	CR–BAA to CR–BAB
	plus one more
737–2B2	5R–MFA
737–2C0	N570GB to N574GB
737–2E1	CF–EPL, CF–EPO and
	CF–EPR
737–	Three for Southern Airlines

Model 747

ONE OF THE most-discussed new aeroplanes of recent years, the Boeing 747 is the first of a new generation of long-range, high-capacity transport aircraft that will see service during the 1970s, and which collectively have become known as 'Jumbo jets'. The need for an aircraft of such elephantine proportions could be seen as long ago as the early 1960s, when charts plotting the probable growth of airline passenger and freight traffic indicated that, by the mid-1970s, this traffic would be such as to require prodigious quantities of 'standard' sized transports—or a new definition of the standard itself. Market research pointed favourably towards the latter course, and by August 1965 Boeing had formed a preliminary design group to study a new, outsize transport aircraft. In March 1966 this became a firm project, with the Boeing Model number 747. It was

offered to the airlines: in the following month, Boeing was able to reveal details publicly with the news that Pan American had placed a conditional order for 25, and in July 1966 the go-ahead for production was given—even though, at that point, the company had not received what it considered a 'safe' number of orders from other airlines.

Quite apart from its physical size, the 'Jumbo' could not be fitted into the existing company manufacturing complex in the Seattle area, which was fully occupied with production of the existing 707/720/727/737 range of jet transports. So, in 1967, Boeing began building a $200m new plant at Everett, some 30 miles north of Seattle. This plant, where production now proceeds of the world's largest airliner, includes the world's largest single-roofed building, which has a volume of 200,000,000cu ft. The sheer size of the aeroplane itself and the programme behind it make it easy to devise

impressive lists of 'firsts' and other superlatives, yet in essence its size is the only outstanding feature of the 747. This, of course, is an over-simplification, but essentially the 747 design contains no magic technological breakthrough or new aerodynamic approach: it is simply a bigger aeroplane, with bigger engines and carrying a bigger payload, than anyone had ever built before for airline service. Its development was based on, and aided by, design work carried out by Boeing when contending for the outsize military transport aircraft requirement that was ultimately met by the Lockheed C–5A Galaxy.

Externally the 747 is as handsomely proportioned as its predecessor, the 707, with nothing but the passenger windows to give it scale when it is in the air. It is inside the cabin that the difference from other airliners is immediately and dramatically apparent, for here the passenger, for the first time, is no longer made to feel that he is travelling in what is in effect an oversized metal tube. The cabin of the 747 is 185ft long, 20ft wide—enough for comfortable eight-abreast seating with two aisles and no passenger more than one seat away from a gangway—and has a maximum 8ft 4in headroom. Basic accommodation is for 374 passengers, with a maximum of 490 possible if ten-abreast seating is used, but in practice airlines have tended so far to work to a figure of around 350, to take

Left: *Roll-out of the first Boeing 747 'Jumbo' jet in 1968.*

Above right: *Boeing 747 Series 100 of Pan American Airways.* [B. M. Service

Right: *First Boeing 747B (747–200) taking off for its initial flight on October 11, 1970.*

full advantage of the customer appeal of the spacious interior. The wings of the 747 have the full complement of lift and control surfaces developed for earlier Boeing airliners, and the great weight of the 'Jumbo' fully loaded is rendered compatible with existing airport runways by the use of an 18-wheel landing gear—a twin-wheel nose unit and a 16-wheel, four-bogie main gear. Power plant is four Pratt & Whitney JT9D series turbofan engines.

Roll-out of the first 747 took place on September 30, 1968, followed by the first flight on February 9, 1969. Five aircraft were used in the certification programme, enabling the 747 to receive FAA type approval on December 30, 1969, and enter service with Pan American between New York and London on January 22, 1970. By April 30, 1971, the airlines had ordered a total of 204 Model 747s, of which 122 had been delivered. Up to early 1971, four basic models of the 747 had been announced. The initial Boeing 747 version, with JT9D–3 engines, is known as the Series 100; the other three, designated 747B, 747C and 747F, are respectively passenger, convertible and cargo models known collectively as the Series 200. These have a 65,000lb increase in gross weight over the Series 100, JT9D–7 engines and carry more fuel, but are otherwise similar except that the 747C and 747F have a hinged nose-cone which opens forward and upward to allow direct loading of cargo on to the main deck. Maximum cargo payloads of the C and F models are 242,928lb and 257,858lb respectively. The first flight of a 747B was made on October 11, 1970, by the 88th production aircraft, one of five ordered by Northwest Orient

Airlines. On November 12, 1970, this aircraft took off at 820,700lb—the highest weight at which any aircraft had been flown up to that time. Initial certification weight of the 747B was 775,000lb. The first exampled of the 747 Series 200 entered service during 1971, with KLM becoming the first operator of this model. During 1970, the Pan American 747s (including three on lease to Eastern) were phased through a modification programme which included structural changes for a gross weight of 735,000lb and the introduction of JT9D-3AW engines. These modified aircraft were called 747As by Pan Am.

Specification (Boeing 747-100)

SPAN	195ft 8in
LENGTH	231ft 4in
HEIGHT	63ft 5in
WING AREA	5,500sq ft
GROSS WEIGHT	710,000lb
MAX SPEED	625mph
CRUISING SPEED	585mph
RANGE with max payload	5,500 miles

Production and Sales (up to April 30, 1971)
Boeing 747-100 Series

747–121	N652PA to N659PA
	N731PA to N744PA
	N747PA to N755PA
	N770PA to N771PA
747–122	N4703U to N4704U
	N4710U to N4714U
	N4716U to N4720U
	N4723U
	N4727U to N4729U
	N4732U, N4735U
747–123	N9661 to N9676
747–124	N26861 to N26864
747–127	N501BN to N502BN
747–128	F–BPVA to F–BPVH
	plus three more
747–129	OO–SGA to OO–SGB
747–130	D–ABYA to D–ABYC
747–131	N93101 to N93109
	N53110 to N53112
	N93113 to N93114
	N93118 to N93119
	plus three more
747–132	N9896 to N9900
747–133	CF–TOA to CF–TOC
747–135	N77772 to N77773
747–136	G–AWNA to G–AWNL
747–143	I–DEMA and I–DEME
747–146	JA8101 to JA8103
747–148	EI–ASI to EI–ASJ
747–151	N601US to N610US
747–156	EC–BRO to EC–BRP

Boeing 747-200 Series

747–206B	PH–BUA to PH–BUG
747–230B	D–ABYD, D–ABYF
	plus two more
747–230F	D–ABYE
747–237B	VT–EBD to VT–EBE
	plus two more
747–238B	VH–EBA to VH–EBD
747–243B	I–DEMO and I–DEMU
	plus one more
747–244B	ZS–SAL to ZS–SAN
	plus two more
747–246B	JA8104 to JA8116
747–251B	N611US to N615US
747–256B	EC–BRQ
747–257B	HB–IGA to HB–IGB
747–258B	4X–AXA to 4X–AXB
747–282B	Two for TAP
747–283B	SE–DDL, OY–KFA
747–200F	One for Korean Airlines

Model 2707–300

ON JUNE 5, 1963, a little more than six months after British and French government and industry representatives signed an agreement to develop the Concorde supersonic transport, President John F. Kennedy initiated a design competition in the United States for an American SST and the engines to power it. Three airframe/engine partnerships bid for this important contract, but that between North American and Curtiss Wright was eliminated in June 1964, leaving as rival contenders Boeing/General Electric and Lockheed/Pratt & Whitney. Lockheed's design, the L–2000, was widely expected to be the winner: its double-delta fixed-wing layout was more straightforward than the swing-wing design proposed by Boeing, implying a shorter development period and lower costs; moreover, Lockheed, with far fewer civil commitments than Boeing, might have been expected to reach the hardware stage sooner, so presenting greater competition to the Concorde.

Consequently when President Johnson, on January 1, 1967, endorsed the FAA's recommendation of the Boeing design, there was a considerable degree of surprise, for it was felt in many quarters that the double technological leap of producing a variable-geometry SST—especially when viewed against the unhappy development record of the F–111 swing-wing fighter—meant, in effect, trying to produce a second-generation SST before any manufacturer or airline had had experience of building or operating a first-generation aircraft of this type.

Nevertheless, Boeing had been undertaking research into supersonic transport design since as early as 1952, albeit at comparatively low priority in view of extensive commitments to its subsonic transport programme. The original submission, known as Model 733, was for a 430,000lb, 150/227-seat aircraft with four separately-podded turbofan engines beneath the wings and designed to cruise at Mach 2·7. Between January 1964 and September 1966 this was superseded by a revised and enlarged design, provisionally called Model 2707, weighing 675,000lb, seating more than 300 passengers and having the engines repositioned—still singly—beneath a much-enlarged horizontal tail. It also introduced, as had the Concorde, an articulated nose section that could be drooped during take-off and landing manoeuvres. Power plant was to be four General Electric GE4/J5P turbojets, each developing 63,200lb st with afterburning.

However, in October 1968, Boeing announced that it had abandoned the swing-wing approach of the 2707–200 altogether, and was concentrating instead on the Model 2707–300, a design with fixed 'gull' wings having a delta-shaped planform. This mounted the GE4 engines (whose predicted take-off thrust, with reheat, was later increased to 68,600lb) directly under the wings and projecting aft of the trailing-edge. The Boeing 2707–300 retained much of the systems design of its predecessor, but was to use sandwich skins instead of machined panels in the wing construction. A contract for the completion of two prototypes was placed in September 1969, and the first of these was due to fly in late 1972 or early 1973, with production scheduled to start in 1975 and entry into airline service in 1978. The first five production aircraft were earmarked for Pan American and TWA (two each) and Alitalia (one). The programme remained, however, subject to the approval of the US Senate, which on March 24, 1971, voted 51–46 against granting a continued appropriation for prototype construction and development. On the following day Boeing and General Electric were instructed to cease their work and that of their sub-contractors immediately.

Plans as announced up to the cancellation were for an eventual family of aircraft covering a variety of payload/range combinations and having fuselages of varying widths and lengths. Typically, these included a 250-seat long-range version with a prototype-size fuselage; one with a 296ft fuselage seating up to 321 passengers; and another with a 298ft fuselage seating 281/298 passengers. Cost of the tremendously expensive prototype and development programme was to have been borne, in the initial stages, chiefly by the US government, which was to recover this money through royalties on the sales of approximately the first 300 aircraft and perhaps beyond. Boeing, General Electric, several customer airlines and major sub-contractors were to participate in a risk-sharing agreement to provide the remainder of the capital needed. Altogether twenty-six airlines had reserved delivery positions (at $200,000 per aircraft) for 122 Boeing 2707–300s.

Specification

SPAN	141ft 8in
LENGTH	286ft 8in
HEIGHT	50ft 1in
WING AREA	8,497sq ft
GROSS WEIGHT	635,000lb
MAX SPEED	1,780mph
CRUISING SPEED	1,780mph
RANGE	About 4,000 miles

Artist's impression of the Boeing 2707–300 projected supersonic transport.

Index/Type and Production List

MODEL NO.	DESIGNATION/NAME	TYPE	BUILT FOR/USER	DATE	NO. BUILT	PAGE
1	B & W	2-seat biplane	New Zealand govt.	1916	2	13
1A	B & W replica	2-seat biplane	Company use	1966	1	13
2	C–4, C–11	2-seat biplane	Company use	1916	1	14
3	C–5, C–6	Training biplane	US Navy	1917	2	14
4	EA	Training biplane	US Army	1917	2	16
5	C–650/700, C–1F, CL–4S	Training biplane	US Navy/W.E. Boeing (C–700)	1917–18	52	14
6	B–1	3-seat flying-boat	Edward Hubbard	1919	1	17
6D, 6E	B–1D, B–1E	4-seat flying-boat	Commercial use	1928	8	17
7	BB–1	3-seat flying-boat	Aircraft Mfg Co	1919	1	19
8	BB–L6	3-seat biplane	H. Munter	1920	1	19
10	GA–1	Armoured attack triplane	US Army	1921	10	20
10	GA–2	Armoured attack biplane	US Army	1922	2	21
15	PW–9/FB series	Fighter biplane	US Army/US Navy	1923–28	131	22
16	DH–4/O2B series	Bomber/Observation biplane	US Army/US Navy	1920–25	298	26
21	NB–1, NB–2	Training biplane	US Navy	1924–25	77	28
40	Model 40	Passenger/mail biplane	Airline/private use	1925–32	81	29

MODEL NO.	DESIGNATION/NAME	TYPE	BUILT FOR/USER	DATE	NO. BUILT	PAGE
42	XCO–7	Observation biplane	US Army	1925	3	26
50	PB–1/XPB–2	Patrol flying-boat	US Navy	1925	1	30
53	FB–2	Fighter biplane	US Navy	1925	2	24
54	FB–4/FB–6	Fighter biplane	US Navy	1924	1	24
55	FB–3	Fighter biplane	US Navy	1925–26	3	24
58	XP–4	High-altitude fighter	US Army	1926	1	31
63	TB–1	Torpedo biplane	US Navy	1927	3	32
64	Model 64	Training biplane	Pacific Air Transport	1926	1	33
66	XP–8	Fighter biplane	US Army	1927	1	33
67	FB–5	Fighter biplane	US Navy	1926–27	27	23
68	AT–3	Advanced training biplane	US Army	1926	1	34
69	F2B–1	Fighter biplane	US Navy	1926–28	35	35
74/77	XF3B–1	Fighter biplane	US Navy	1927	1	35
77	F3B–1	Fighter biplane	US Navy	1928	73	35
80	Model 80	Passenger transport biplane	BAT/Standard Oil	1928–30	16	37
81	XN2B–1, Model 81A	Training biplane	US Navy/Commercial	1928	2	39
83	XF4B–1	Fighter biplane	US Navy	1928	1	39
89	XF4B–1	Fighter biplane	US Navy	1928	1	39

MODEL NO.	DESIGNATION/NAME	TYPE	BUILT FOR/USER	DATE	NO. BUILT	PAGE
93	XP–7	Fighter biplane	US Army	1928	1	48
95	Model 95	Passenger/mail biplane	Commercial	1928–29	25	48
96	XP–9	Fighter monoplane	US Army	1930	1	49
99	F4B–1	Fighter biplane	US Navy	1929	27	39
100	Model 100	1/2-seat biplane	Commercial/test	1929–32	8	46
101	XP–12A	Fighter biplane	US Army	1929	1	40
102	P–12, P–12B	Fighter biplane	US Army	1929–30	99	40
103–199		Allocated to Boeing aerofoil sections				
200	Monomail	Mail/cargo monoplane	Commercial	1930	1	50
202	XP–15	Fighter monoplane	US Army	1930	1	52
203	Model 203	Training biplane	Commercial	1929–36	7	53
204	Models 204, 204A	5-seat flying-boat	Commercial	1929–30	7*	17
205	XF5B–1	Fighter monoplane	US Navy	1930	1	52
214	Y1B–9	Bomber monoplane	US Army	1931	1	54
215	YB–9	Bomber monoplane	US Army	1931	1	54
218	Model 218	Fighter biplane	Demonstrator	1930	1	41
221	Monomail	Passenger/cargo monoplane	Commercial	1930	1	51

* 2 by Boeing, 4 by Boeing-Canada, 1 private; also 1 Totem by Boeing-Canada.

MODEL NO.	DESIGNATION/NAME	TYPE	BUILT FOR/USER	DATE	NO. BUILT	PAGE
222	P–12C	Fighter biplane	US Army	1931	96	41
223	F4B–2	Fighter biplane	US Navy	1931	46	41
226	Model 226	Passenger transport biplane	Commercial	1930	1	38
227	P–12D	Fighter biplane	US Army	1931	35	41
234	P–12E	Fighter biplane	US Army	1931–32	110	42
235	F4B–3, F4B–4	Fighter biplane	US Navy	1931–33	114	43
236	XF6B–1/XBFB–1	Fighter biplane	US Navy	1933	1	56
246	Y1B–9A	Bomber monoplane	US Army	1932–33	5	54
247	Model 247	Passenger transport monoplane	Commercial	1933–35	75	56
248	XP–936, P–26	Fighter monoplane	US Army	1932	3	58
251	P–12F	Fighter biplane	US Army	1932	25	43
256	'1932' F4B–4	Fighter biplane	Brazilian Air Force	1932	14	46
264	XP–940, YP–29	Fighter monoplane	US Army	1934	3	61
266	P–26A, P–26B, P–26C	Fighter monoplane	US Army	1934–35	136	59
267	Model 267	Fighter biplane	Brazilian Air Force	1933	9	46
273	XF7B–1	Fighter monoplane	US Navy	1933	1	62
281	Model 281	Fighter monoplane	China/Spain	1934–35	12	60

MODEL NO.	DESIGNATION/NAME	TYPE	BUILT FOR/USER	DATE	NO. BUILT	PAGE
294	XB–15	Long-range heavy bomber monoplane	US Army	1937	1	62
299	B–17 Flying Fortress	Long-range bomber monoplane	US Army	1935–45	6,981*	64
307	Stratoliner	Passenger transport monoplane	PAA/TWA/Hughes	1937–40	10	71
314	Model 314	Passenger transport flying-boat	PAA	1938–41	12	74
344	XPBB–1 Sea Ranger	Long-range patrol flying-boat	US Navy	1942	1	86
345	B–29 Superfortress	Long-range heavy bomber monoplane	US Army	1942–46	2,756†	87
345	B–50 Superfortress	Long-range heavy bomber monoplane	USAF	1947–53	371	92
367	C–97, KC–97	Transport and tanker	USAF	1944–56	888	94
377	Stratocruiser, 'Guppy' series	Passenger transport	Commercial	1947–50	56	97/8
400	XF8B–1	Fighter/attack	US Navy	1944–45	3	101
450	B–47 Stratojet	Medium-range strategic bomber	USAF	1947–56	1,373‡	101
451	XL–15, YL–15 Scout	Liaison/observation	US Army	1947–49	12	105

* Plus 3,000 by Douglas and 2,750 by Vega.
† Plus 668 by Bell and 536 by Martin.
‡ Plus 294 by Lockheed and 274 by Douglas; one additional B–47B by Lockheed not completed.

MODEL NO.	DESIGNATION/NAME	TYPE	BUILT FOR/USER	DATE	NO. BUILT	PAGE
464	B–52 Stratofortress	Long-range strategic bomber	USAF	1952–62	744	106
500–599		Allocated to gas-turbine engines and Industrial Products Division				
600–699		Allocated to Pilotless Aircraft Division				
707	Model 707	Passenger/cargo transport	Commercial	1954–	*	110/6/9
717	KC–135, C–135	Tanker and transport	USAF	1956–65	806	112
720	Model 720	Passenger/cargo transport	Commercial	1959–68	154	118
727	Model 727	Passenger/cargo transport	Commercial	1962–	*	129
733	Model 733	Initial SST designation of 1964–66				
737	Model 737	Passenger/cargo transport	Commercial	1967–	*	132
739	RC–135	Reconnaissance	USAF	1965–66	14	112
747	Model 747	Outsize passenger/cargo transport	Commercial	1968–	*	134
2707-300†	Model 2707–300	Supersonic passenger transport				136

Stearman Models						
75	Kaydet series	Training biplane	US Army/US Navy	1936–45	8,584	76
X–90	XBT–17	Training monoplane	US Army	1941	1	83

* Still in production at time of closing for press; see text for total up to April 30, 1971.
† Provisional designation, outside of normal sequence.

MODEL NO.	DESIGNATION/NAME	TYPE	BUILT FOR/USER	DATE	NO. BUILT	PAGE
X–91	XBT–17	Training monoplane	US Army	1941	1(cvtd)	83
X–100	XA–21	Attack bomber	US Army	1939	1	84
X–120	XAT–15 Crewmaker	Aircrew trainer	US Army	1942	2	85

Vertol Models (continuing original Piasecki sequence: not integrated with Boeing Model number sequence)

107	Model 107–II/H–46 Sea Knight	Transport helicopter	Commercial/US Navy	1958–	see text	123
114	CH–47 Chinook	Transport helicopter	US Army/Italy/Iran	1961–	see text	126
347	Model 347	Experimental helicopter	Boeing/US Army	1970	1	127

Other types built by Boeing

—	Curtiss HS–2L	Patrol flying-boat	US Navy	1918	25	16
—	Thomas-Morse MB–3A	Fighter biplane	US Army	1921–22	200	22
—	Blackburn Shark III	Torpedo-spotter-reconnaissance biplane	RCAF	1937	17	70
—	Douglas DB–7B, A–20C	Attack bomber/trainer	RAF/USAAF	1941–42	380	81
—	Waco CG–4A	Troop/cargo glider	USAAF	1942	750	82
—	Consolidated PBY, PB2B	Patrol flying-boat	RAF/RAAF/RNZAF/ US Navy	1942–45	362	82